W9-APK-759

Entertaining
THOUGHTS...

A lighthearted collection of recipes, menus,
and entertaining tips presented by
The Junior League of the Lehigh Valley

Entertaining
THOUGHTS...

A lighthearted collection of recipes, menus,
and entertaining tips presented by
The Junior League of the Lehigh Valley

Published by The Junior League of the Lehigh Valley

The cookbook is a collection of favorite recipes,
which are not necessarily original recipes.

Copyright © 2001 by
The Junior League of the Lehigh Valley, Inc.
2200 Avenue A, Suite 101
Bethlehem, Pennsylvania 18017

LC Control Number: 00 131130
ISBN: 0-9700215-0-X

Edited, Designed, and Manufactured by
Favorite Recipes® Press
an imprint of

FRP

P.O. Box 305142
Nashville, Tennessee 37230

Art Director and Book Design: Steve Newman
Project Manager: Ginger Ryan Dawson

Manufactured in the United States of America
First Printing: 2001
10,000 copies

THE LEHIGH VALLEY

Our expansive community of 600,000 is located in the heart of northeastern Pennsylvania—just 55 miles from Philadelphia and 85 miles from New York City. The Pocono Mountains, home to ski resorts and lakeside cottages, are just 30 minutes away. Small towns and friendly faces dot the landscape between the three largest cities in the Valley: Allentown, Bethlehem, and Easton.

In 1998, *Money* magazine ranked the Lehigh Valley the 15th most livable community in the Northeast. No doubt, the editors took into consideration our cultural offerings, historic preservation efforts, natural resources, educational facilities, and recreational activities.

Among the many places to savor in the Lehigh Valley are the Allentown Art Museum, State Theatre, and Zoellner Arts Center. Sports fans quickly find their way to the Lehigh Valley Velodrome and the Nazareth Speedway. There are parks, pools, and walking paths near the Lehigh River that runs through us. And there are nine colleges and universities, including two community colleges, which enrich us through public lectures, performances, and exhibits.

For more information and what to do and see in the Lehigh Valley, contact the Lehigh Valley Convention and Visitors Bureau at 800-747-0561 or visit us on the web at www.lehighvalleypa.org.

ENTERTAINING THOUGHTS

...of more than 150 delicious and delectable recipes
from which to choose
...about a cheesecake worthy of the finest New York bakery
...of the perfect wine to complement tonight's entrée
...concerning menus for the casual, and the not-so-casual,
get-together
...of a cookbook created to serve not only families
but an entire community

We have all entertained. And we have all entertained thoughts about how to host the ultimate gathering—with panache and with ease. In this book we share our favorite recipes along with tips and ideas to enhance your get-together. We offer creative and delicious menus and some regional information about our community and the ways in which we live, work, play, give— and entertain—all year long.

Many thanks are due to the membership of The Junior League of the Lehigh Valley and to spouses, families, and friends for giving their recipes, taste buds, patience, and support.

And special thanks to you, the cook and consummate entertainer, for purchasing this book. Your purchase enables The Junior League of the Lehigh Valley to persevere in its mission: to strengthen families by working in the community to promote education, to assist families in need, and to fight violence and abuse in the home.

With our gratitude and good wishes,

The Cookbook Committee

TABLE OF CONTENTS

WHO WE ARE

We started in 1922—as the Junior Welfare League of Bethlehem, Pennsylvania—small, but purposeful.

In those early years, we equipped the new milk kitchen in the Children's Ward of St. Luke's Hospital, started the hospital's library, founded The Children's Theatre with the local AAUW and Jr. Women's Club, presented a "Books" series on the local radio station, and hired a kindergarten teacher and, later, an occupational therapist for the Children's Ward.

Our interest in literacy and children has remained steadfast during the last three quarters of a century, though our membership, and our name, has grown.

In 1943, we became the Junior League of Bethlehem, and 25 years later, we changed our name to The Junior League of the Lehigh Valley (JLLV) to reflect the geographic diversity of our membership and the dynamic, burgeoning community around us.

We funded other community projects over the years through JLLV grants, shared our volunteer expertise and "hands on" training with boards of local organizations, founded a neighborhood center, led the charge for drug education and environmental studies, championed the cause of the physically challenged, promoted literacy and education, and began a Center for Health Education.

Our collaboration with other not-for-profits enabled us to build a second safe haven for an invaluable and oversubscribed domestic violence shelter, to create an interactive science education center for children, to bring dynamic educational exhibits to the community where children and their parents could learn and discover together, and to lay the foundation for a Children's Advocacy Center.

Throughout this book—amidst the recipes and food for thought—you'll learn more about our service to this community and the volunteer spirit that nourishes us.

The Cookbook Committee

Nancy Kesling Westwood, Chair
Sally Murphy Albano, Sustaining Advisor
Jolene D. Carey
Danielle Lamie Foder
Sara Levin
Megan O'Hara Malicki
Linda Wolf McLinden
Maureen Barber Schenkel
Kathleen Duggan Trimble

Marketing Committee

Kathleen Duggan Trimble, Chair
Jolene D. Carey
Cynthia M. DiRenzo
Julie Jordan
Nancy Kesling Westwood

The Purveyors of Truth

Every recipe in this book was prepared and tasted by one of eleven tasting groups. We truly believe that the success of this book relies solely on the integrity of the recipes herein, so every effort was made to ensure that the recipes provided are clearly written, easy to follow, and delicious to taste.

7

KIDS ON THE BLOCK

A long-standing project of the Junior League, Kids on the Block is a program designed to teach school-age children about the differences and similarities between each of us. Our volunteers take three puppets with different skin colors and mental and physical challenges into the schools. Through a scripted play, we show children how to be compassionate and how to appreciate the gifts that each of us has to share.

To date, we've introduced "the Kids" to thousands of school-children and, we hope, to a world filled with greater tolerance and understanding.

I Had A Lovely Time
AT YOUR PARTY

Football Championships Party

JANUARY

Football Punch

Tortilla Wraps

Spicy Shrimp

Sweet and Salty Almonds

White-Lights-on-the-Parkway Chili

Red Cabbage and Mango Salad

Mexican Corn Bread

Nana's Walnut Brownies

Oatmeal Cranberry Cookies

Help your guests get into the team spirit by using cloth or purchased napkins at your buffet in the colors of the two opposing squads.

Move several TVs into the entertaining area so everyone can get "50-yard-line" seats.

Serve light snacks and appetizers during the pregame show and have the rest of your buffet ready by halftime. Keep your beverage area well stocked throughout the game, brewing coffee and tea just after halftime. Offer desserts in the fourth quarter.

Mexican Corn Bread

3 eggs, beaten
1 (14-ounce) can cream-style corn
5 teaspoons baking powder
2 cups small curd cottage cheese
1 cup melted shortening
2 cups yellow cornmeal
1½ teaspoons salt
2 (7-ounce) cans whole chile peppers
1½ cups shredded Cheddar cheese

Combine the eggs, corn, baking powder, cottage cheese,
shortening, cornmeal and salt in a large bowl and mix until smooth.
Pour half the batter into a greased 9×13-inch baking pan.
Rinse the chile peppers and pat dry. Layer the chile peppers, half the
Cheddar cheese and the remaining batter in the prepared pan.
Top with the remaining cheese. Bake at 350 degrees for 1 hour or
until the edges begin to brown. Let cool before cutting.
Yield: 12 servings.

Winter Snow Day Lunch

FEBRUARY

Hot chocolate, warm cider and hot toddies
Red Onion and Goat Cheese Tart
Applejack Pork and Sauerkraut
Harvest Corn Pudding
Spinach Medley with Red Wine Vinaigrette
Fresh baked artisan bread
Praline Apple Pie

Serve hot chocolate in oversize, earthenware mugs. Have a big bowl of marshmallows and a selection of flavored extracts on hand.

Consider serving lunch around the coffee table in front of the fireplace. Have your guests sit on pillows near the fire.

Cinnamon and spice-scented candles also set the mood from the kitchen. Or, add some scented kindling to the fire. Be careful not to over-scent the room. You want your food to be the most fulfilling aroma.

*Denotes a menu item not included in this book.
Prepare your favorite version.

Love Knot Napkin Fold

Open napkin to full size. Fold napkin in half, bringing bottom edge to top. (Illus. 1) Bring upper and lower edge to meet in center. Bring lower edge to top edge. (Illus. 2) Leaving a little more than half at left, turn right side under and down. (Illus. 3) Turn left side over so that its side comes along that of right segment. (Illus. 4) Bring left side of napkin over so that it is perpendicular to other segment. (Illus. 5) Lift lower segment over top one. (Illus. 6)

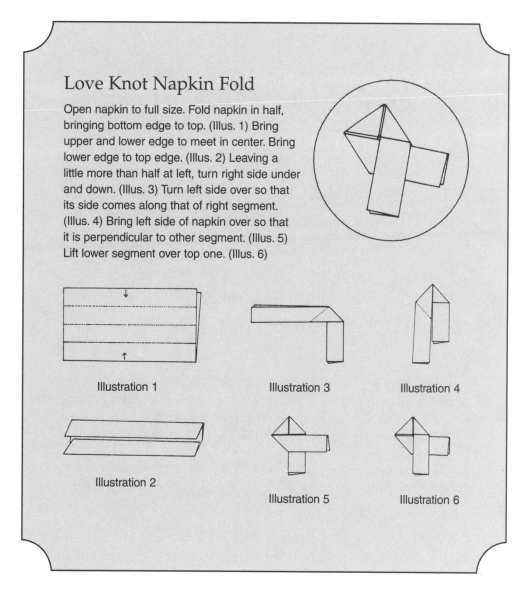

Illustration 1

Illustration 3

Illustration 4

Illustration 2

Illustration 5

Illustration 6

Luck O' the Irish Dinner
MARCH

*Bass or Harp Ale, Irish Whiskey Sours
Creamed Mussels with Whiskey and Wine
Strip Steak with Pale Ale and Shallot Sauce
Scalloped Potatoes with Leeks
Irish Soda Bread
Walnut Lemon Meringue Bombe

Celebrate the true Irish colors by incorporating more than just green in your decor. Add orange and white to your color scheme. Use all three colors in your napkin selection, or tie green, orange, and white ribbons around the napkins at each place.

Use miniature shamrock plants in a long, natural basket as your centerpiece. Or place a miniature plant at each tablesetting, noting your guests' places around the table.

Don't get too caught up in the green beer and glittered hats—that is more an American tradition than Irish. The Irish are known for their enthusiastic hospitality and warmth. Spend your energies in making your guests feel welcome in your home and appreciated in your life.

Invest in some traditional Irish CDs to play as background music while you dine. If you really want to splurge, hire a clogger or Irish dancer to entertain and engage your guests after dinner.

*Denotes a menu item not included in this book.
Prepare your favorite version.

Ascot Napkin Fold

With napkin open to full size, fold in half, bringing bottom point up to top. Fold in half again, bringing bottom fold to top fold; crease and release. (Illus. 1) Fold bottom up midway to crease. (Illus. 2) Bring bottom to crease made in center of triangle. (Illus. 3) Turn up fold once more. (Illus. 4) Turn right point to left of top point. (Illus. 5) Turn left point to right of top point. (Illus. 6)

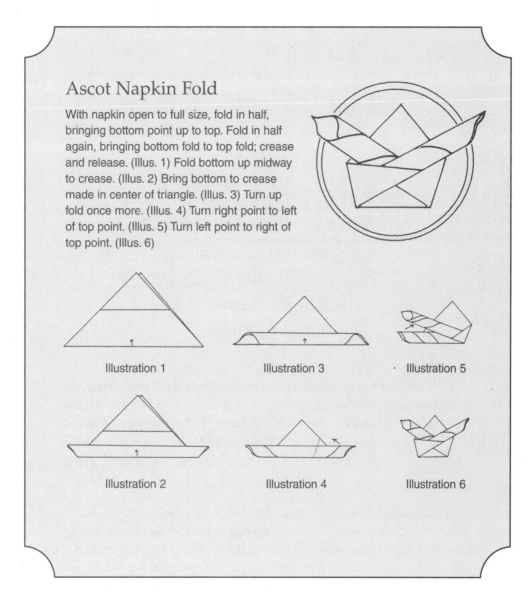

Illustration 1

Illustration 3

Illustration 5

Illustration 2

Illustration 4

Illustration 6

Egg Hunt Brunch

APRIL

Mimosas with freshly squeezed juices
Fruit Salsa with Cinnamon Tortilla Crisps
Asparagus Frittata
Rise-and-Shine Salmon Quiche
Treacle Scones
Blueberry Kuchen

For a twist on traditional mimosas, mix 1 cup sliced strawberries with $1/4$ cup orange juice and $1/8$ cup Grand Marnier. Then place 2 tablespoons of this mixture in Champagne glasses and pour Champagne on top. Slice a strawberry down the middle (not all the way through) and place on rim of Champagne glass. Cheers!

Place pastel-dyed Easter eggs in large, clear glass bowls for a colorful centerpiece. Or, three weeks prior to your hunt, line an Easter basket with a plastic bag and fill with potting soil and plant grass seeds. Remember to water. At party time, place dyed eggs in the grass and use as your centerpiece. Potted tulips in full bloom also add color and beauty to your table. About $1/3$ of the way down the stem of the tulip bunch, tie a pastel organza ribbon into a bow.

*Denotes a menu item not included in this book.
Prepare your favorite version.

Rabbit Napkin Fold

With napkin open to full size, fold in half, bringing top edge to bottom edge. (Illus. 1) Fold in half again on dotted line, bringing top fold to bottom. (Illus. 2) Find center by bringing two sides together, creasing and opening again. Bring right and left sides to meet in center. (Illus. 3) Lay bottom right raw edges on middle crease. (Illus. 4) Fold right side in half on dotted line, bringing right to center and making an ear. (Illus. 5) Repeat 4 and 5 on left side. (Illus. 6) Fold top point down in back. (Illus. 7) Tuck center point into back pocket. (Illus. 8) Set on table for finished rabbit. (Illus. 9)

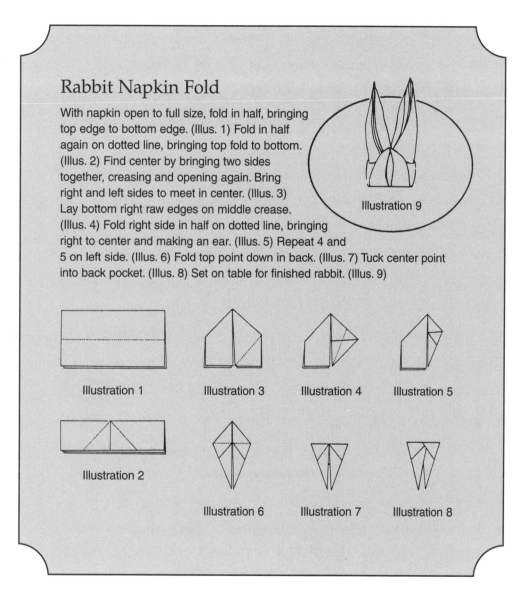

Illustration 9

Illustration 1

Illustration 3

Illustration 4

Illustration 5

Illustration 2

Illustration 6

Illustration 7

Illustration 8

Derby Day Party on the Lawn

MAY

Mint Juleps
Smoked Trout Pâté
Pesto Cheesecake
Fillet of Beef
Roquefort Potato Gratin
Red Leaf Lettuce with Raspberry Vinaigrette
Marinated Asparagus
Chocolate Chip Bourbon Pecan Pie

Use silver mint julep cups to hold flowers for your centerpieces and use sprigs of mint for greens in the arrangements.

Encourage your female guests to wear their favorite, or wildest, hats. Have other guests select a winner or two and offer flowers or other treats as prizes for their fashion (non!)sense.

Send out invitations with a horse theme. Horseshoes (call your local stable or riding school for availability) make clever place markers. Permanent markers will identify your guests' seats at the table.

Mint Juleps

16 lemons
3 cups sugar
3 cups water
$1/2$ cup sugar
1 lemon, cut into wedges
Mint sprigs
Ice
3 cups bourbon

Squeeze the juice from 16 lemons into a bowl and reserve the peels.
Combine 3 cups sugar and water in a small saucepan and cook until the
sugar dissolves, stirring constantly. Add the reserved lemon peels and
cook for 15 minutes or until the mixture is syrupy. Let cool. Pour $1/2$ cup
sugar on a small plate. Rub the lemon wedges along the rims of frosted
glasses or silver julep cups and dip the rims into the sugar to coat.
Crush a mint sprig in the bottom of each glass with a wooden spoon.
Place a lemon wedge in each glass and fill with ice. Pour $1/2$ cup
of the syrup and 3 tablespoons of the lemon juice in each glass.
Top with $1/2$ cup bourbon. Garnish with additional mint.
Yield: 6 servings.

Wedding Attendants' Lunch

JUNE

*Champagne, cranberry spritzers
Salmon Terrine
Chicken and Orange Salad
Crab Meat Potato Salad with Warm Saffron Dressing
League Board Party Salad
*Bread basket assortment
Strawberry Kiwifruit Tart with Mint Custard

For a simple centerpiece that becomes a favor for your guests, plant seasonal flowers (begonias, pansies, primroses) in small terra-cotta pots and tie white organza ribbon in a bow around the pots. Group the flowerpots together in the center of the tables as decorations and then invite each guest to take one home.

Send a blank recipe card with each invitation and ask each guest to fill it out with a recipe he/she would like to pass along to the bride. As guests bring recipes to the shower, the recipes can be placed in an attractive recipe box for the bride's keeping.

Create a small scrapbook in advance. Have the attendants and wedding party guests share special memories, marital advice, and good wishes. Prepare the book as a pre-wedding gift for the bride to share with her new husband.

*Denotes a menu item not included in this book.
Prepare your favorite version.

Flower Holder Napkin Fold

With napkin open to full size, fold in half, bringing up the left side from the bottom. Fold in half again on dotted line, bringing up right side from bottom. (Illus. 1) Turn down three points, each one higher than the last. (Illus. 2) Turn right and left corners under in thirds. (Illus. 3)

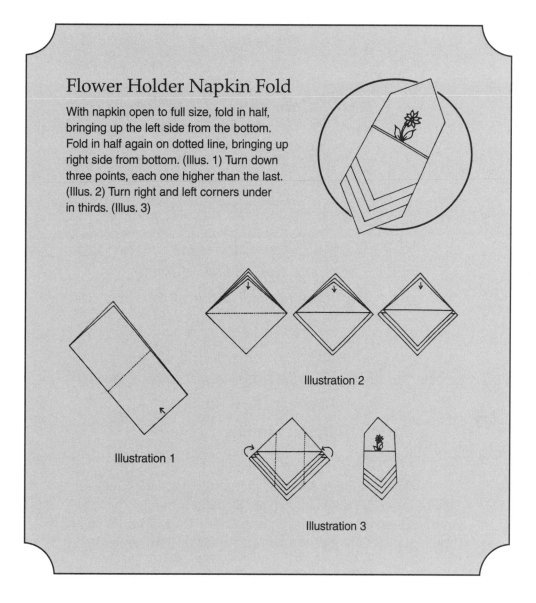

Illustration 1

Illustration 2

Illustration 3

21

Celebration of Summer Picnic Lunch

JULY

*Lemonade and freshly brewed iced tea
Black Bean and Corn Salsa, Hummus
Indian Summer Sangria
Barbecued Spareribs
Lemon Coleslaw, Baked Butter Beans
New Potato Salad with Bacon and Mustard Seeds
Buttermilk Biscuits
Nostalgic Strawberry Pie

Use this menu for your Memorial Day, 4th of July, or Labor Day celebration and create a patriotic theme. Purchase inexpensive red, white, and blue dish towels and use them as place mats or line baskets with them for chips, biscuits, etc.

Also, you can buy children's sand pails in these colors and serve salads in them or, use as a centerpiece, filling with sand and placing small flags in them.

Blueberries and strawberries with whipped cream carry out the color scheme and provide a fruity addition to dessert.

*Denotes a menu item not included in this book.
Prepare your favorite version.

Buttermilk Biscuits

2 cups flour
1 tablespoon baking powder
³/4 teaspoon salt
¹/2 teaspoon baking soda
5 tablespoons shortening, chilled
1 cup buttermilk

Sift the flour, baking powder, salt and baking soda into a
large bowl. Cut in the shortening until crumbly. Add the buttermilk,
stirring with a fork until a soft dough forms. Knead lightly on a
floured surface. Roll the dough out to ³/4-inch thickness.
Cut with a biscuit cutter. Place the biscuits on a baking sheet.
Bake at 425 degrees for 12 to 15 minutes or until golden brown.
Yield: 12 servings.

Back-to-School Coffee

SEPTEMBER

Gourmet coffees and teas
Jewish Apple Cake
Almond Biscotti
*Fresh fruit salad
Chocolate Toffee Bark
Salmon Terrine with bagels

For a simple centerpiece, fill a large wood or pottery bowl with apples (an apple for the teacher).

Have each mother bring school supplies purchased when shopping with her own children and donate them to a homeless shelter that serves families.

Plan to get together more frequently throughout the year! These get-togethers are a great opportunity to arrange car pools, share PTA duties, coordinate babysitting— and to give Mom a break.

Write your menu on a small chalkboard, or have a few miniature slates on hand to place at each guest's seat.

*Denotes a menu item not included in this book.
Prepare your favorite version.

Clown's Hat Napkin Fold

With napkin open to full size, fold in half, bringing bottom of napkin to top. (Illus. 1) Holding point (A) carefully with thumb, roll (B) loosely over and up to center (C) without creasing. (Illus. 2) Continue rolling cone. (Illus. 3) Turn napkin upside down. Turn up hem all around. Back view. (Illus. 4)

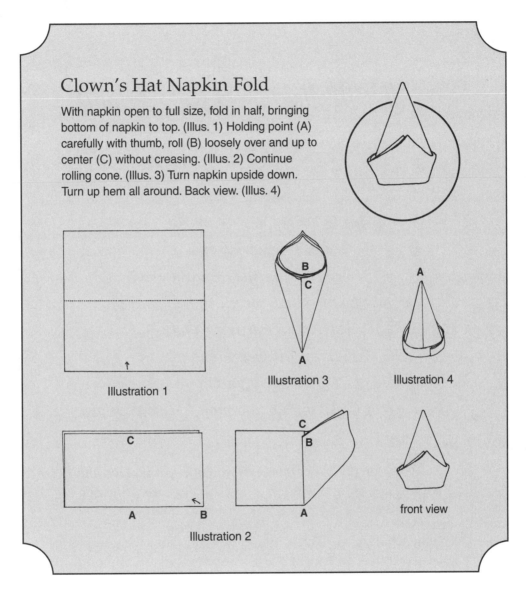

Illustration 1

Illustration 2

Illustration 3

Illustration 4

front view

25

All Hallow's Eve Dinner

OCTOBER

*Autumn beers
"Bobbing for Apples" Pumpkin Dip
Black-Eyed Susans
Curried Chutney Spread
Fall Foliage Vegetable Stew served in hollowed pumpkins
Rich and Charlie's Salad
Savory Mashed Potatoes
*French baguette
Pear Apple Crisp with Cinnamon Crème Anglaise

Fill a long bread basket with miniature pumpkins and gourds, apples, and walnuts—you can also use a dressier bowl for a less rustic look for your centerpiece.

Decorate a half-mask (covering the eyes only) for each guest as a place card. Let each guest wear it and/or then take it home.

Play background music that reflects the spirit of the season (avoid the howls and yells and go for a classical selection).

*Denotes a menu item not included in this book.
Prepare your favorite version.

All Hallow's Eve Stew

Small pumpkins
Hot stew, such as Fall Foliage Vegetable Stew (page 153)
Puff pastry
1 egg
1 tablespoon water

De-cap and hollow out the small pumpkins and fill with the
hot stew. Roll the puff pastry into rounds approximately 2 inches bigger
than the pumpkin openings. Top each pumpkin with a pastry
round. Use a cookie cutter to cut out leaf, bat or cat shapes from the
puff pastry. Place the pastry cut-outs on top of the pastry and
brush with a mixture of the egg and water. Poke a small hole in
the top of each to allow steam to escape. Bake in a 450-degree oven
for 5 minutes or until the top is golden brown.
Yield: variable.

Home for the Holidays Dinner

NOVEMBER

*Beaujolais

Roasted Butternut Squash Bisque

*Roast Turkey

Oyster Stuffing

Sweet Potato Soufflé

Seven-Vegetable Casserole

Cranberry Apple Salad

Walnut Torte

Mrs. Savell's Carrot Cake with Cream Cheese Frosting

Apple Streusel Cheesecake

Serve a few light nibbles with cocktails before dinner—but nothing too heavy (you want people to stuff themselves on turkey, not hors d'oeuvre!). Some suggestions—crudités, an assortment of olives, or a wheel of Brie cheese with cranberry chutney on top baked in the oven for a few minutes to warm the Brie.

Use your finest serving pieces. This is a time to give thanks for being together—why not show your guests how much you appreciate them?

*Denotes a menu item not included in this book.
Prepare your favorite version.

Four Feathers Napkin Holder

With napkin open to full size, fold in half diagonally, bringing up bottom corner to top. (Illus. 1) Place finger on center bottom of napkin (A). Working with top layer only, bring top corner (B) down and across to (C), folding on dotted line. (Illus. 2) Again, working only with top layer, bring top corner (D) down and across to (E), folding on dotted line. (Illus. 3) Working with both layers of napkin, bring top corner (F) down and across to (G), folding on dotted line. (Illus. 4) Turn top corner under and to back, folding on dotted line. (Illus. 5) It should look like this. (Illus. 6) Fold bottom point under and place in goblet.

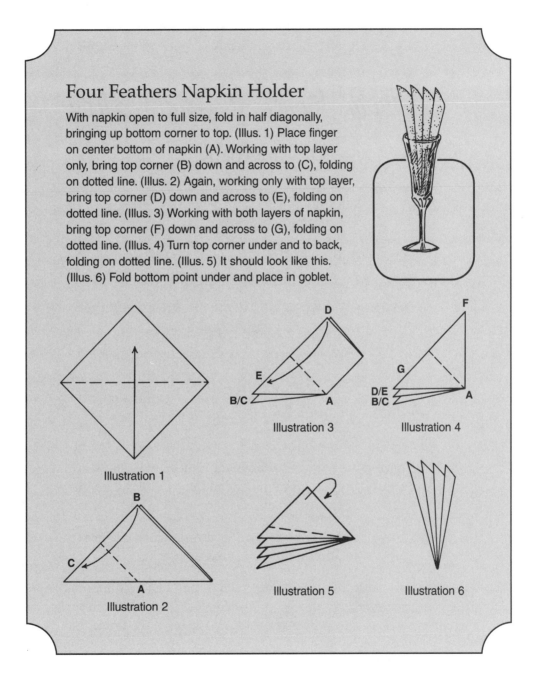

Illustration 1

Illustration 2

Illustration 3

Illustration 4

Illustration 5

Illustration 6

29

Holiday Cheer Cocktail Party

DECEMBER

*Champagne or mulled wine
Clam Oreganato Dip
Bacon and Water Chestnut Wraps
Jeweled Cheese Ball, Spinach Quenelles
Roasted Red Pepper and Artichoke Tapenade
Bleu Cheese Puffs
*Smoked Turkey with rolls and condiments
*Cheese and antipasto tray
Rum Balls, Virginia Fudge, Chambord Brownies

A roaring fire is great for ambiance but may be too warm for a large party. Instead, place pillar candles of varying heights in the fireplace to provide atmosphere without the heat.

Many breweries have special winter brews. These make a nice addition to your holiday bar.

A simple but elegant flower arrangement is holly and white roses. You can place evergreen swags in the center of your table and tuck gold or silver painted pinecones and white rose in the branches.

Try to incorporate the different religious traditions of your friends to make them feel welcome.

*Denotes a menu item not included in this book.
Prepare your favorite version.

Buffet Napkin Fold

With napkin open to full size, fold in half, bringing up the left side from the bottom. (Illus. 1) Fold in half again on dotted line, bringing up right side from bottom. (Illus. 2) Four points are at top. Roll down top layer. (Illus. 3) Fold opposite corners under. (Illus. 4) Insert silverware into pocket. (Illus. 5)

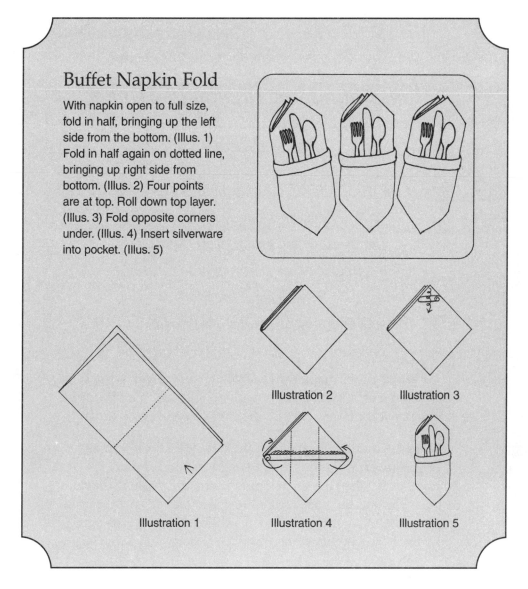

Illustration 1

Illustration 2

Illustration 3

Illustration 4

Illustration 5

Christmas Morning Brunch

DECEMBER

*Poinsettia Cocktails (Champagne and cranberry juice)
Moravian Sugar Cake
Fabulous Ham and Cheese Soufflé
The Lafayette Inn's Homemade Granola
Strawberry Bread
Christmas Morning Ambrosia

With a glitter marker (available at craft stores), write each guest's name on a plain glass ornament. Resting on a pine sprig or against the coffee cup, these make colorful place cards.

Consider hosting this breakfast the day *AFTER* Christmas—December 26. In the United Kingdom, this holiday is Boxing Day—when the festivities are past and presents have to be put away and the boxes stored for next year. It's a wonderful opportunity to continue the mood a little longer by welcoming neighbors and others whose families already may have left.

*Denotes a menu item not included in this book.
Prepare your favorite version.

Christmas Morning Ambrosia

6 cups orange sections
3 cups shredded coconut
3 cups chopped fresh pineapple
1 1/2 cups maraschino cherry halves, rinsed, drained
3/4 cup chopped pecans
Confectioners' sugar to taste

Combine the oranges, coconut, pineapple and cherries
in a large bowl and mix well. Stir in the pecans.
Stir in the desired amount of confectioners' sugar.
Chill, covered, until serving time.
Yield: 12 servings.

DONE IN A DAY

Volunteers serve their communities in the limited hours they have to spare. The JLLV, wanting to maximize the amount we give back to our community, has designed a series of one-day projects, or those that can be "done in a day," every month.

We stock canned goods and boxes at the Food Bank. We help our local Meals on Wheels program with deliveries and food shopping. We read books for the sight-impaired. We collect baby items for the women's shelter. We "Race for the Cure" with others fighting the war against breast cancer. We spend time with young girls at the youth center, celebrating the holidays and making crafts. And, sometimes, we just lend an ear to listen.

From Brunch
TO LUNCH

Fruit Salsa with Cinnamon Tortilla Crisps

Fruit Salsa
2 *Granny Smith apples,*
    peeled and chopped
1 *cup chopped strawberries*
1 *kiwifruit, chopped*
Juice of 1 orange
2 *tablespoons brown sugar*
2 *tablespoons apple jelly*

For the salsa, combine the apples, strawberries and kiwifruit in a bowl and mix gently. Stir in the orange juice. Add the brown sugar and jelly and mix well.

Cinnamon Tortilla Crisps
Flour tortillas
Cinnamon and sugar
    to taste

For the crisps, cut each tortilla into 8 thin strips. Spray lightly with water. Sprinkle with cinnamon and sugar. Arrange in a single layer on a baking sheet. Bake at 400 degrees for 8 to 10 minutes or until light brown and crisp. Serve with the salsa.
Yield: 16 servings.

Smoked Salmon Dip

4 ounces smoked salmon,
    shredded
1/3 cup cream
1/2 teaspoon capers
1/8 teaspoon freshly
    ground pepper
Tabasco sauce to taste
1 large cucumber,
    thinly sliced
Rye rounds

Combine the salmon, cream, capers, pepper and Tabasco sauce in a blender or food processor container. Process until smooth. Spoon into a serving bowl. Sprinkle with additional pepper. Serve with the cucumber rounds and crackers. Yield: 12 to 16 servings.

Praline-Crowned Brie

1 (15-ounce) round Brie
    cheese
1/2 cup chopped pecans
1/4 cup packed brown sugar
1 tablespoon Cognac or
    maple syrup
Whole strawberries
    (optional)

Arrange the cheese in a round baking dish. Sprinkle with the pecans. Pat the brown sugar over the top and drizzle with the Cognac. Bake at 350 degrees for 20 to 25 minutes or until the top is slightly caramelized and the Brie is heated through but not runny. Top with the strawberries. Serve immediately with assorted unsalted party crackers. Yield: 10 to 12 servings.

The Lafayette Inn's Homemade Granola

From the Lafayette Inn, Easton

3 cups rolled oats
1/2 cup wheat germ
1/2 cup slivered almonds
1/2 cup chopped pecans
1/2 cup chopped walnuts
1/2 cup unsalted sunflower kernels
1/2 cup chunky peanut butter
1/3 cup honey
1 teaspoon vanilla extract
1/4 teaspoon cinnamon
1 cup golden raisins
1 cup dried cranberries

Combine the oats, wheat germ, almonds, pecans, walnuts and sunflower kernels in a bowl and mix well. Heat the peanut butter, honey, vanilla and cinnamon in a saucepan over low heat until mixed, stirring frequently. Add to the oats mixture and mix well.

Spread the oats mixture evenly on a baking sheet. Bake at 300 degrees for 20 minutes. Remove from oven; stir. Let stand until cool. Stir in the raisins and cranberries. Store in an airtight container. Yield: 8 cups.

Chile Brunch Eggs

1/3 cup flour
2 teaspoons salt
2 teaspoons pepper
2 teaspoons minced garlic or garlic salt
1 teaspoon baking powder
10 to 12 eggs, beaten
1 pound Monterey Jack cheese, shredded
2 cups cottage cheese
1 (4-ounce) can diced mild chiles, drained
1/4 cup (1/2 stick) butter, melted

Combine the flour, salt, pepper, garlic and baking powder in a bowl and mix well. Combine the eggs, Monterey Jack cheese, cottage cheese, chiles and butter in a bowl and mix well. Stir in the flour mixture.

Spoon into a 9×12-inch baking dish. Bake at 350 degrees for 45 minutes. Yield: 10 servings.

Creative Containers

Use household items instead of vases to display flowers to carry out the theme for your table. For example: teapots for an afternoon tea, aluminum watering cans for a garden luncheon, silver bowls for a bridal shower or anniversary. Baskets, wine glasses, and terra-cotta flowerpots are also clever ideas.

Scottish Farmhouse Eggs

1½ cups fresh white bread crumbs
3 tablespoons chopped fresh chives or
    green onions
3 ounces Dunlop, sharp Cheddar or
    Cheshire cheese, shredded
4 eggs
Salt and cayenne pepper to taste
2 cups half-and-half
Fresh chives, coarsely chopped

Coat the bottom and side of a 9-inch round baking dish with butter. Sprinkle half the bread crumbs over the bottom of the baking dish. Top with 1½ tablespoons chives and half the cheese.

Break the eggs carefully over the prepared layers, spacing evenly. Sprinkle with the remaining bread crumbs, 1½ tablespoons chives, remaining cheese, salt and cayenne pepper. Pour the half-and-half over the top.

Bake at 350 degrees for 20 minutes or until the eggs are almost set. Sprinkle with coarsely chopped chives. Serve immediately. Yield: 4 to 6 servings.

Asparagus Frittata

8 ounces fresh asparagus
5 eggs
1 cup milk
1 small onion, chopped
1 teaspoon salt
1/2 teaspoon basil
1/8 teaspoon white pepper
8 ounces Swiss cheese, shredded

Steam the asparagus just until tender-crisp; drain. Plunge
into ice water in a bowl to stop the cooking process; drain.
Cut the asparagus into 1-inch pieces. Arrange the
asparagus in a greased round baking dish.

Whisk the eggs in a bowl until blended. Add the milk and
mix well. Stir in the onion, salt, basil and white pepper. Add
the cheese and mix well. Pour over the asparagus. Bake at
350 degrees for 30 minutes or until a knife inserted 1 inch
from the edge comes out clean.

For Broccoli Frittata, substitute broccoli for the asparagus
and Cheddar cheese for the Swiss cheese and omit the
basil. Yield: 8 servings.

Crab Meat Quiche

1 unbaked (10-inch) deep-dish pie shell
2 cups flaked drained backfin crab meat
1/2 cup thinly sliced green onions with tops
1/2 cup evaporated milk
2 tablespoons flour
2 or 3 eggs, beaten
1/2 cup mayonnaise
1 teaspoon Worcestershire sauce
1/4 teaspoon dry mustard
8 ounces Swiss cheese, shredded

Prick the bottom and side of the pie shell with a fork. Bake
at 450 degrees for 8 minutes. Remove to a wire rack to
cool. Reduce the oven temperature to 350 degrees.

Combine the crab meat and green onions in a bowl
and mix well. Stir in the evaporated milk and flour. Add
the eggs and mix well.

Combine the mayonnaise, Worcestershire sauce and dry
mustard in a bowl and mix well. Stir into the crab meat
mixture. Add the cheese and mix well. Spoon into the pie
shell. Place on a baking sheet. Bake for 45 minutes or until
set. Yield: 8 servings.

Rise-and-Shine Salmon Quiche

1 unbaked frozen (10-inch) deep-dish pie shell
1 (16-ounce) can salmon
Light cream
1/4 cup minced or chopped onion
2 tablespoons chopped pimentos
2 tablespoons chopped fresh parsley
1/4 teaspoon poultry seasoning
Pepper to taste
2 tablespoons butter
4 eggs, beaten

Let the pie shell stand at room temperature for 20 minutes. Prick the bottom with a fork. Drain the salmon, reserving the liquid. Combine the reserved liquid in a measuring cup with just enough light cream to measure 2 cups.

Sauté the onion, pimentos, parsley, poultry seasoning and pepper in the butter in a nonstick skillet for 3 to 4 minutes or until the onion is tender. Combine the onion mixture and cream mixture with the eggs in a bowl and mix well. Flake the salmon into the pie shell. Pour the egg mixture over the salmon.

Bake at 350 degrees until set or until a knife inserted in the center comes out clean. Yield: 8 servings.

Fabulous Ham and Cheese Soufflé

16 slices white bread, crusts trimmed, cubed
1 pound ham, cubed
4 cups cubed sharp Cheddar cheese
1½ cups cubed Swiss cheese
3 cups milk
6 eggs
½ teaspoon onion salt
½ teaspoon dry mustard
3 cups crushed cornflakes
¼ cup (½ stick) butter, melted

Arrange half the bread cubes over the bottom of a 9-inch quiche pan or round baking dish. Layer with the ham, Cheddar cheese and Swiss cheese. Top with the remaining bread cubes.

Whisk the milk, eggs, onion salt and dry mustard in a bowl until blended. Pour over the prepared layers. Chill, covered, for 8 to 10 hours. Sprinkle with a mixture of the cornflakes and butter.

Bake at 375 degrees for 40 minutes or until set. You may substitute 1 pound cooked crumbled sausage for the ham. Yield: 8 to 10 servings.

Substitutions

For	Substitute
1$^1/2$ teaspoons cornstarch	1 tablespoon flour
1 ounce unsweetened chocolate	3 tablespoons baking cocoa plus 1 tablespoon butter
1 cup honey	1$^1/4$ cups sugar plus $^1/4$ cup liquid
1 cup buttermilk	1 tablespoon cider vinegar or lemon juice plus enough milk to equal 1 cup
1 cup half-and-half	1 cup evaporated milk

Broccoli and Tomato Casserole

1$^1/2$ cups chopped broccoli
2 medium tomatoes, chopped
2 cups shredded Cheddar cheese
1 cup shredded Monterey Jack pepper cheese
1 cup milk
3 eggs
$^1/4$ cup flour
$^1/2$ teaspoon salt

Layer the broccoli, tomatoes, Cheddar cheese and
Monterey Jack pepper cheese in an ungreased 9-inch
baking dish. Whisk the milk and eggs in a bowl until
blended. Add the flour and salt and mix well. Pour over the
prepared layers. Bake at 375 degrees for 30 minutes or
until set. Serve with salsa. Yield: 8 to 10 servings.

Chicken and Orange Salad

2¹/2 cups cubed cooked
    chicken
4 navel oranges, separated
    into sections
1 red onion, thinly sliced
12 black olives
¹/8 teaspoon minced fresh
    rosemary
¹/2 cup lemon juice
¹/4 cup olive oil
³/4 teaspoon salt
¹/2 teaspoon pepper

Combine the chicken, orange sections, onion, olives and rosemary in a bowl and mix gently. Whisk the lemon juice, olive oil, salt and pepper in a bowl. Add to the chicken mixture and toss to coat. Marinate, covered, in the refrigerator for several hours before serving. You may substitute one 6- to 8-ounce can mandarin oranges for the navel oranges.
Yield: 4 to 6 servings.

Curried Chicken Salad

3 boneless skinless chicken
    breasts
2 tablespoons mayonnaise
1¹/2 teaspoons (heaping)
    mango chutney
¹/2 teaspoon curry powder
Salt and pepper to taste
1 to 2 tablespoons baking
    raisins or plumped
    raisins
Shredded coconut
    (optional)
Finely chopped peanuts
    (optional)

Cook the chicken in enough water to cover until cooked through. Let cool slightly and coarsely chop. Combine the chicken, mayonnaise, chutney and curry powder in a bowl and mix well. Season with salt and pepper. Stir in the raisins. Spoon into a serving bowl. Sprinkle with coconut and/or peanuts.

Serve as a salad, stuff into a pita pocket, roll in a tortilla or spoon into a puff pastry tart shell.
Yield: 6 to 8 servings.

Crab-Stuffed Avocados

4 large ripe avocados, peeled, cut into halves
1/2 cup lime juice
1 cup mayonnaise
3 tablespoons chopped fresh chives
1/2 teaspoon salt
1/4 teaspoon freshly ground pepper
1 pound lump crab meat, drained
Boston lettuce
3 tablespoons drained capers
Pimento-stuffed green olives

Brush all surfaces of the avocados with some of the lime juice. Cut 2 of the halves into cubes. Combine the remaining lime juice, mayonnaise, chives, salt and pepper in a bowl and mix well. Discard any pieces of shell or cartilage from the crab meat, taking care not to break up the lumps. Fold the crab meat and cubed avocado into the mayonnaise mixture.

Line a serving platter with Boston lettuce. Arrange the avocado halves over the lettuce. Mound some of the crab meat mixture in each avocado half. Top with the capers and olives. Yield: 6 servings.

Marinated Tortellini

24 to 32 ounces frozen cheese tortellini
3/4 cup olive oil
1/2 cup grated Romano or Parmesan cheese
1/4 cup wine vinegar
1 teaspoon minced onion
2 garlic cloves, minced
Basil to taste
Parsley flakes to taste
Oregano to taste
Grated Romano or Parmesan cheese to taste

Cook the tortellini using package directions until al dente; drain. Rinse the pasta with cold water to stop the cooking process; drain.

Whisk the olive oil, 1/2 cup cheese, wine vinegar, onion, garlic, basil, parsley flakes and oregano in a bowl.

Add the tortellini and toss gently to coat. Sprinkle with cheese to taste. Chill, covered, until serving time. Serve chilled or at room temperature. Yield: 6 to 8 servings.

Vidalia and Arugula Sandwiches

3 large Vidalia onions, cut into 1/2-inch slices
1/2 cup extra-virgin olive oil
1/2 teaspoon coarse salt
1/2 teaspoon freshly ground pepper
3 large sprigs of rosemary
4 large sprigs of thyme
1/2 cup mayonnaise
2 large whole grain buns, split, toasted
2 bunches arugula, stems removed
Coarse salt to taste
Freshly ground pepper to taste

Arrange the onions in a shallow dish. Combine the olive oil, 1/2 teaspoon coarse salt, 1/2 teaspoon pepper, rosemary and thyme in a bowl and mix well. Pour over the onions. Marinate, covered with plastic wrap, at room temperature for 45 minutes to 24 hours, turning once; drain. Grill the onions over hot coals or broil for 6 to 8 minutes or just until tender and slightly blackened.

Spread the mayonnaise on the cut sides of the buns. Layer the arugula and sliced onions over the mayonnaise on 2 halves. Sprinkle with coarse salt and pepper to taste. Top with the remaining bun halves.

You may substitute kaiser rolls or thickly sliced homemade bread for the whole grain buns. Cut the sandwiches into halves and serve as appetizers or as a snack.
Yield: 2 to 4 servings.

Bread Machine Challah

7 ounces hot (120 degrees) water
1/4 cup honey
1/4 cup (1/2 stick) butter, melted
2 eggs
3 1/4 tablespoons flour
1 tablespoon dry yeast
1 1/2 teaspoons salt
1 egg
2 tablespoons milk

Combine the hot water, honey, butter, eggs, flour, yeast and salt in a bread machine using manufacturer's directions. Set your machine on the dough cycle. Check the dough during the kneading cycle, adding additional flour if required. Remove the dough from the bread machine. Punch the dough down, adding additional flour if needed to make an easily handled dough.

Divide the dough into 3 equal portions. Roll each portion between your hands into a 10 1/2- to 11-inch-long tapered rope. Pinch and tuck the top ends of the ropes under and braid down, pinching and tucking the bottom under. Arrange the braid on a nonstick baking sheet. Let rise, covered loosely with foil, for 30 to 35 minutes or until doubled in bulk.

Whisk the egg and milk in a bowl until blended. Brush the braid with the egg mixture. Bake at 350 degrees until the bread is golden brown and feels hollow when lightly tapped. Yield: 10 servings.

Crème Brûlée French Toast

1 (8- or 9-inch) loaf country-style bread or challah
$1/2$ cup (1 stick) unsalted butter
1 cup packed brown sugar
2 tablespoons corn syrup
5 eggs
1 teaspoon vanilla extract
1 teaspoon orange liqueur
$1/4$ teaspoon salt

Cut the bread loaf into 1-inch slices, discarding the end pieces. Trim the crusts. Combine the butter, brown sugar and corn syrup in a saucepan. Cook until smooth, stirring frequently. Pour into a 9×13-inch baking pan. Arrange the bread slices over the brown sugar mixture, overlapping the slices if necessary.

Whisk the eggs, vanilla, liqueur and salt in a bowl. Pour over the prepared layers. Chill, covered, for 8 to 24 hours. Bring to room temperature.

Bake at 240 degrees for 35 to 40 minutes or until puffed and golden brown. Invert the slices onto a serving platter. Yield: 8 to 10 servings.

Natural Candleholders

Hollow out miniature pumpkins, gourds, or artichokes to hold votive candles for your table. You can also put tea lights in a martini glass for a different look.

Irish Soda Bread

2 cups flour
2 tablespoons sugar
2¹/4 teaspoons baking soda
2¹/4 teaspoons baking powder
1 teaspoon salt
3 tablespoons unsalted butter
1 cup buttermilk
¹/2 cup raisins
2 tablespoons caraway seeds
1 tablespoon unsalted butter, melted

Combine the flour, sugar, baking soda, baking powder and
salt in a bowl and mix well. Cut in 3 tablespoons butter
until crumbly. Add the buttermilk, raisins and caraway
seeds, stirring just until moistened. Shape the mixture into
a ball.

Knead on a lightly floured surface for 1 minute. Shape
into a ball and pat into a round flat loaf on an ungreased
baking sheet. Brush with 1 tablespoon melted butter. Bake
at 350 degrees for 30 minutes. Cut into wedges.
Yield: 8 to 10 servings.

Strawberry Bread

1¹/₂ cups fresh strawberries, sliced
1¹/₄ cups vegetable oil
5 eggs, beaten
3 cups flour
2 cups sugar
1 tablespoon cinnamon
1 teaspoon baking soda
1 teaspoon salt
1¹/₄ cups pecans, chopped

Combine the strawberries, oil and eggs in a bowl and mix well. Sift the flour, sugar, cinnamon, baking soda and salt into a bowl and mix well. Stir the flour mixture into the strawberry mixture. Add the pecans and mix well.

Spoon the batter into 2 greased and floured 5×9-inch loaf pans. Bake at 350 degrees for 1 hour or until a wooden pick inserted in the center comes out clean. Cool in pans for 10 minutes. Remove to a wire rack to cool completely.

You may substitute 2 thawed 10-ounce packages frozen strawberries for the fresh strawberries. Yield: 16 servings.

Jewish Apple Cake

4 red apples, peeled, sliced
4 teaspoons sugar
2 teaspoons cinnamon
4 eggs
2 cups sugar
1 cup vegetable oil
3 cups flour
1 tablespoon baking soda
1/2 teaspoon salt
1/2 cup orange juice
1 teaspoon vanilla extract

Toss the apples, 4 teaspoons sugar and cinnamon in a bowl. Whisk the eggs in a bowl until blended. Stir in 2 cups sugar and oil. Stir in a mixture of the flour, baking soda and salt; the batter will be stiff. Add the orange juice and vanilla and mix well.

Grease a 10-inch tube pan. Spoon 1/3 of the batter into the prepared pan. Spread with 1/2 of the apple mixture. Layer with 1/2 of the remaining batter and the remaining apple mixture. Top with the remaining batter.

Bake at 350 degrees for 1 hour and 20 minutes to 1 1/2 hours or until the cake tests done.
Yield: 10 to 12 servings.

Blueberry Kuchen

1 cup flour
2 tablespoons sugar
1/2 cup (1 stick) butter
1 tablespoon vinegar
3 cups fresh blueberries
1/2 cup sugar
2 tablespoons flour
1/8 teaspoon cinnamon
1 cup fresh blueberries

Combine 1 cup flour and 2 tablespoons sugar in a bowl. Cut in the butter until crumbly. Add the vinegar, stirring until the mixture forms a ball. Pat the dough over the bottom and up the side of a greased 9-inch pie plate.

Combine 3 cups blueberries, 1/2 cup sugar, 2 tablespoons flour and cinnamon in a bowl and mix gently. Spoon the blueberry mixture into the pastry-lined pie plate.

Bake at 350 degrees for 45 minutes. Sprinkle with 1 cup blueberries. Serve warm. Yield: 8 servings.

Chocolate Banana Soy Shake

Combine 8 ounces chocolate soy milk and 1 sliced frozen banana in a blender container. Process until smooth. Substitute vanilla soy milk for the chocolate soy milk and add 1 envelope instant hot chocolate mix to increase the calcium content.
Yield: 1 serving.

Moravian Sugar Cakes

2 or 3 small potatoes
1¹/₂ envelopes dry yeast
1 cup sugar
¹/₂ cup shortening
1 teaspoon salt
2 eggs
4 cups flour
Margarine
Cinnamon to taste
Nutmeg to taste
Brown sugar to taste

Combine the potatoes with enough water to cover in a saucepan. Bring to a boil. Boil until tender. Drain, reserving 1 cup of the liquid. Mash the potatoes. Cool the reserved liquid to lukewarm. Stir in the yeast.

Beat the sugar, shortening and salt in a mixing bowl until creamy. Beat in the eggs until blended. Stir in 1 cup of the mashed potatoes; store the remaining mashed potatoes in the refrigerator for another use. Add half the flour and mix well. Stir in the yeast mixture and remaining flour. Knead lightly; the dough will be sticky. Divide the dough into 2 equal portions. Pat the dough into 2 greased 8×8-inch baking pans. Let rise for 3 to 10 hours. Dot with margarine.

Mix cinnamon, nutmeg and brown sugar in a bowl. Sprinkle over the prepared layers. Bake at 350 degrees for 10 to 15 minutes or until light brown. Serve warm. You may freeze, covered, for future use. Reheat before serving. Yield: 16 to 18 servings.

Treacle Scones

2 cups flour
1/4 cup packed dark brown sugar
2 1/2 teaspoons baking powder
1/2 teaspoon baking soda
1/4 teaspoon cinnamon
1/4 teaspoon nutmeg
1/4 teaspoon salt
1/2 cup dried currants
1/4 cup (1/2 stick) unsalted butter
2 tablespoons treacle or dark molasses
3/4 cup buttermilk
Melted butter
Sugar to taste

Sift the flour, brown sugar, baking powder, baking soda, cinnamon, nutmeg and salt into a bowl and mix well. Stir in the currants. Combine the butter and molasses in a saucepan. Cook over low heat until blended, stirring frequently. Remove from heat. Stir in the buttermilk. Add the buttermilk mixture to the flour mixture and stir just until moistened.

Knead the dough gently on a generously floured surface for 20 minutes or until smooth. Divide the dough into 2 equal portions. Pat each portion into a 5-inch round. Cut each round into 4 wedges. Arrange the wedges 2 inches apart on an ungreased cookie sheet. Brush with melted butter. Sprinkle with sugar. Bake at 425 degrees for 20 minutes or just until firm. Serve hot with whipped cream and preserves. Do not use blackstrap molasses in this recipe. Yield: 8 scones.

CHILDREN'S THEATRE OF BETHLEHEM

Since 1935, the Children's Theatre of Bethlehem has been setting a grand stage for children and their families in the Lehigh Valley with three professionally produced plays each year. Tickets are priced affordably so all families can participate.

In addition, the Children's Theatre sponsors an annual, three-day School Play for first- and second-grade students from local school districts. More than 3,000 children, on average, attend the performances.

The Junior League of the Lehigh Valley co-founded this program with area representatives of the American Association of University Women (AAUW) and the Junior Women's Club. This is just one of the enduring community collaborations of the JLLV.

Happy Happy HOURS

Black Bean and Corn Salsa

2 tomatoes
1 (15-ounce) can black beans, rinsed and drained
1 (10-ounce) package frozen corn, thawed
1 cup chopped Spanish onion
1/2 cup finely chopped fresh cilantro
Juice of 2 limes
1 tablespoon olive oil
2 teaspoons minced garlic
3/4 teaspoon Tabasco sauce
1/2 teaspoon cumin
1/2 teaspoon salt
1/2 teaspoon pepper

Peel, seed and finely chop the tomatoes. Combine the tomatoes with the black beans, corn and onion in a large bowl.

Add the cilantro, lime juice, olive oil and garlic and mix well. Stir in the Tabasco sauce, cumin, salt and pepper. Chill, covered, for 2 to 10 hours. Serve with tortilla chips. Yield: 36 servings.

Clam Oreganato Dip

2 (7-ounce) cans chopped clams
1 tablespoon lemon juice
1 large onion, chopped
½ cup (1 stick) butter
2 garlic cloves, minced
1 tablespoon parsley
1 tablespoon oregano
2 dashes of Tabasco sauce
1 pinch of red pepper flakes
½ cup Italian-style bread crumbs
⅓ cup grated Parmesan cheese
Paprika to taste

Combine the clams and lemon juice in a bowl and set aside. Sauté the onion in the butter in a skillet until tender. Add the garlic, parsley, oregano, Tabasco sauce, red pepper flakes, bread crumbs and cheese. Mix until well coated. Remove from heat and toss with the clams.

Spoon into a baking dish. Sprinkle with paprika. Bake at 350 degrees for 20 minutes. Serve immediately with assorted crackers or bread. Yield: 18 to 24 servings.

Crudités

Scoop out the center of red cabbage, small pumpkins, red peppers, or small loaves of bread to hold vegetable dip. Line a basket with gourmet lettuces, put the dip holders in, and then stuff veggies around it. Be creative! Use string beans, snow peas, asparagus, jicama, yellow squash, baby corn, and other non-traditional veggies.

Chile con Queso

2 eggs
1/4 cup milk
2 (4-ounce) cans chopped
    green chiles, drained
1 cup shredded Swiss
    cheese
1 cup shredded Cheddar
    cheese
1 cup shredded Monterey
    Jack cheese

Whisk the eggs and milk in a bowl. Add the chiles and mix well. Stir in the Swiss cheese and Cheddar cheese. Pour into an 8-inch square dish. Top with the Monterey Jack cheese.

Bake at 350 degrees for 30 minutes or until brown and bubbly. Serve with assorted crackers.
Yield: 16 to 18 servings.

"Bobbing for Apples" Pumpkin Dip

1 cup cooked fresh pumpkin
    or canned pumpkin
16 ounces cream cheese,
    softened
1 cup packed brown sugar
2 tablespoons maple syrup
2 teaspoons cinnamon
Apple slices

Beat the pumpkin and cream cheese in a mixing bowl. Add the brown sugar, maple syrup and cinnamon and beat until smooth.

Serve immediately or chill for up to 24 hours. Does not keep well for a longer period. Serve with apple slices and/or ginger cookies.
Yield: 24 to 30 servings.

Roasted Red Pepper and Artichoke Tapenade

1 (7-ounce) jar roasted red bell peppers,
*   drained and chopped*
1 (6-ounce) jar marinated artichoke hearts,
*   drained and chopped*
1/2 cup finely chopped fresh parsley
1/2 cup grated Parmesan cheese
1/3 cup olive oil
1/4 cup drained capers
3 tablespoons minced garlic
1 tablespoon lemon juice

Combine the bell peppers, artichoke hearts, parsley, cheese, olive oil, capers, garlic and lemon juice in a blender container. Process until well blended and the bell peppers and artichoke hearts are finely chopped.

Spoon into a serving bowl. Serve with pita bread, bagel chips or sliced French bread. You may prepare the tapenade 1 day in advance. Yield: 24 servings.

Bleu Cheese and Olive Ball

8 ounces cream cheese,
    softened
4 ounces bleu cheese,
    crumbled
1/2 cup (1 stick) butter,
    softened
2/3 cup chopped black olives
3 to 4 bunches scallions,
    finely chopped

Combine the cream cheese, bleu cheese and butter in a large bowl and mix until well blended. Stir in the black olives and scallions. Shape into a ball.

Wrap in plastic wrap and chill until serving time. Roll in chopped parsley or walnuts immediately before serving. Serve with assorted crackers. Yield: 36 servings.

Jeweled Cheese Ball

8 ounces cream cheese,
    softened
4 ounces bleu cheese,
    crumbled
2 cups shredded Cheddar
    cheese
2 teaspoons dry sherry or
    apple juice
1/2 teaspoon Worcestershire
    sauce
Seeds of 1 pomegranate,
    or 3/4 cup quartered
    cranberries

Combine the cream cheese, bleu cheese and Cheddar cheese in a bowl and mix well. Mix in the sherry and Worcestershire sauce. Chill, covered, for at least 4 hours. Shape into a ball.

Wrap in plastic wrap and chill for 2 hours or for up to 1 week. Press the seeds or cranberries into the cheese ball. Garnish with parsley. Serve with assorted crackers and melba toast rounds. Yield: 18 to 24 servings.

Curried Chutney Spread

1 (6-ounce) jar ginger
    chutney
16 ounces cream cheese,
    softened
3 tablespoons curry powder
1 teaspoon salt
Green tops of 3 scallions,
    sliced
10 slices bacon, crisp-
    cooked, crumbled
$1/4$ cup chopped smoked
    almonds

Process the chutney in a food processor until smooth. Remove and set aside. Combine the cream cheese, curry powder and $1/6$ of the chutney in the food processor container and process until smooth.

Spread the cream cheese mixture in the bottom of a quiche dish. Spread the remaining chutney on top. Top with the scallions. You may prepare the chutney spread 1 day in advance. Top with the bacon and almonds immediately before serving. Serve with water crackers or melba toast.
Yield: 30 servings.

Hummus

1 (16-ounce) can chick-peas
3 tablespoons tahini paste
1 garlic clove
3 tablespoons lemon juice
1 teaspoon pepper
Olive oil
Paprika

Drain most but not all of the liquid from the chick-peas. Combine the chick-peas, tahini paste, garlic, lemon juice and pepper in a food processor container. Process until smooth.

Spread the dip onto a serving plate. Drizzle with olive oil and sprinkle with paprika. Serve with pita bread cut into quarters. Yield: 16 to 18 servings.

Pesto Cheesecake

Parmesan Crust
1 tablespoon butter,
    softened
1/4 cup dried bread crumbs
2 teaspoons finely grated
    Parmesan cheese

For the crust, butter the bottom and side of a 9-inch springform pan. Combine the bread crumbs and Parmesan cheese in a small bowl. Spread the mixture over the bottom of the pan.

Filling
16 ounces cream cheese
1 cup ricotta cheese
1/2 cup grated Parmesan
    cheese
1/4 teaspoon salt
1/8 teaspoon cayenne
    pepper
3 eggs
1/2 cup prepared pesto
1/4 cup roasted sliced pine
    nuts or pecans

For the filling, beat the cream cheese, ricotta cheese, Parmesan cheese, salt and cayenne pepper in a mixing bowl until creamy.

Add the eggs 1 at a time, beating well after each addition. Mix in the pesto. Pour the mixture into the prepared pan, smoothing the top. Sprinkle with the pine nuts.

Bake at 325 degrees for 45 minutes or until set. Chill, tightly covered, for 8 to 10 hours. Place on a serving plate, loosen edge with a knife and remove the side of the pan. Serve with assorted crackers. Yield: 18 to 24 servings.

Salmon Terrine

1 (15-ounce) can salmon,
    drained
8 ounces cream cheese
1 teaspoon lemon juice
2 teaspoons chopped green
    onions
1/2 teaspoon horseradish
1/2 teaspoon salt
1/8 teaspoon pepper
Chopped pecans

Combine the salmon and cream cheese in a bowl and mix until well blended. Mix in the lemon juice, green onions, horseradish, salt and pepper.

Shape into a ball and wrap in plastic wrap. Chill for 8 to 10 hours. Roll in the chopped pecans immediately before serving. Serve with assorted crackers. Yield: 18 to 24 servings.

Smoked Trout Pâté

1 (8-ounce) package
    smoked trout
1/2 cup mayonnaise
2 tablespoons horseradish
2 tablespoons chopped
    onion
1 hard-cooked egg, chopped
1 tablespoon lemon juice
Salt to taste
Pepper to taste

Process the trout in a food processor until crumbly. Combine the trout, mayonnaise, horseradish, onion, egg, lemon juice, salt and pepper in a bowl and mix well. Spoon into a serving bowl. Serve with assorted crackers.

This pâté is best if prepared 1 day in advance. Yield: 10 to 12 servings.

Sun-Dried Tomato Spread with Cayenne Toasts

Cayenne Toasts

1 loaf French bread, cut into
    1/4-inch slices
1 cup olive oil
2 teaspoons cayenne pepper
1 1/2 teaspoons salt
1 1/2 teaspoons sugar
1/2 teaspoon finely ground
    black pepper
1 teaspoon paprika
1 1/2 teaspoons garlic
    powder
1 1/2 teaspoons onion
    powder

Sun-Dried Tomato Spread

1 1/2 ounces sun-dried
    tomatoes
1 cup olive oil
2 garlic cloves
2 parsley sprigs
5 basil leaves
1/2 teaspoon salt
1/4 teaspoon cayenne pepper
1/8 teaspoon sugar
1 green onion, coarsely
    chopped
2 (4-ounce) rounds goat
    cheese

For the cayenne toasts, place the bread slices on a baking sheet. Whisk the olive oil, cayenne pepper, salt, sugar, black pepper, paprika, garlic powder and onion powder in a bowl until well blended. Whisk the mixture often while using to prevent seasonings from settling. Coat 1 side of each piece of bread with the mixture using a pastry brush. Bake at 200 degrees for 1 hour or until very crisp. The texture should be similar to melba toast. Cool on wire racks. Store in an airtight container until serving time or for up to 2 days. You may freeze for up to 2 months. To recrisp, bake at 350 degrees for 5 to 7 minutes.

For the spread, steam the tomatoes over simmering water for 45 minutes or until rehydrated and completely soft. Combine the tomatoes, olive oil, garlic, parsley, basil, salt, cayenne pepper, sugar and green onion in a glass jar with a tight-fitting lid. Shake to blend well. Chill for 2 days.

Pour into a food processor container. Process until almost smooth, leaving some texture. Place the goat cheese on a serving plate and pour the spread over the cheese. Serve with Cayenne Toasts. Yield: 12 to 18 servings.

Sweet and Salty Almonds

¹/₂ cup (1 stick) butter
1 cup sugar
¹/₈ teaspoon red pepper
1 pound almonds
1¹/₂ teaspoons salt

Melt the butter in a saucepan over medium heat. Add the sugar and red pepper and increase the heat. Cook for 30 seconds. Stir in the almonds. Cook for 5 minutes or until the mixture browns and the almonds begin to pop, stirring constantly. Pour onto a baking sheet and stir in the salt. Serve immediately or store in an airtight container. Yield: 24 servings.

Bacon and Water Chestnut Wraps

1 pound hickory smoked
*   bacon*
1 (8-ounce) can whole
*   water chestnuts,*
*   drained*
¹/₂ cup packed brown sugar
Juice of 1 lemon
2 tablespoons soy sauce
2 tablespoons ketchup

Cut each bacon slice into halves. Wrap ¹/₂ slice bacon around each water chestnut and secure with a wooden pick. Place in a baking dish. Combine the brown sugar, lemon juice, soy sauce and ketchup in a bowl and mix well. Pour the mixture over the bacon-wrapped water chestnuts.

Marinate, covered, in the refrigerator for 3 to 10 hours. Bake at 350 degrees for 15 to 20 minutes or until the bacon is crispy. Yield: 24 to 30 servings.

Black-Eyed Susans

1 cup shredded sharp Cheddar cheese
$1/2$ cup (1 stick) butter
1 cup flour
2 tablespoons finely shredded Parmesan cheese
$1/4$ teaspoon salt
$1/8$ teaspoon red pepper
32 pitted whole dates, halved lengthwise
64 whole blanched almonds
$1/2$ cup (1 stick) butter, melted
Freshly ground black pepper

Process the Cheddar cheese and $1/2$ cup butter in a
food processor until well blended. Add the flour, Parmesan
cheese, salt and red pepper gradually, processing until
well blended. Form the mixture into 2 logs 1 inch in
diameter. Freeze, covered with plastic wrap, for 3 to
4 minutes.

Stuff each date half with an almond and set aside. Slice
the logs into $1/2$-inch slices. Place an almond-stuffed date
in the center of each slice. Wrap the edges up around the
almond-stuffed date; do not enclose the date completely.

Place on a baking sheet and brush with the melted butter.
Sprinkle with black pepper. Bake at 350 degrees for
10 minutes or until light golden brown. Serve warm.
Yield: 64 servings.

Bleu Cheese Puffs

16 ounces cream cheese, softened
1 cup mayonnaise
1 tablespoon minced onion
1/4 cup minced fresh chives
3 to 4 ounces bleu cheese, crumbled
1/2 teaspoon cayenne pepper
1 loaf whole wheat bread, thinly sliced
Paprika to taste

Combine the cream cheese and mayonnaise in a bowl and mix well. Stir in the onion, chives, bleu cheese and cayenne pepper. Cut the bread slices into 1$\frac{1}{2}$- to 2-inch rounds using a cookie cutter.

Spread 1 tablespoon of cheese mixture onto each bread round. Place on a baking sheet and freeze, covered, for at least 1 hour or for up to 2 days.

Bake at 350 degrees for 15 minutes. Sprinkle with paprika and serve immediately. Yield: 24 to 36 servings.

Ambiance

Remember to set the mood. Lighting, candles, flowers, music, and scents are all important. Use low-wattage bulbs in your dining room and entertaining area. Add candles of mixed heights and widths to enhance your gathering. Remember to pay attention to what scent candles you are buying. Unscented is best for the dinner table as it doesn't compete with the taste of the food.

Red Onion and Goat Cheese Tart

2 medium red onions
3 tablespoons olive oil
Salt and pepper to taste
1 sheet frozen puff pastry,
    thawed
1 egg, lightly beaten
8 ounces soft goat cheese
1/4 cup pesto
1/4 cup heavy cream
3 tablespoons chopped
    fresh basil

Cut each onion into 12 wedges. Toss the onions with the olive oil in a bowl. Season with salt and pepper. Place on a baking sheet in a single layer. Bake at 400 degrees for 25 minutes or until the bottoms are golden brown and the onions are tender. Cool on a wire rack.

Roll the pastry on a lightly floured surface into a 10×13-inch rectangle, reserving the pastry trimmings. Place on a baking sheet. Brush the edges of the pastry with some of the beaten egg. Arrange the pastry trimmings along the edge of the tart to form a border. Press gently to seal the edges. Pierce the bottom of the pastry several times with a fork. Bake at 400 degrees for 15 minutes or until the edges of the pastry are golden brown. Cool on a wire rack. Loosen the pastry from the baking sheet. Let cool completely.

Combine the goat cheese, pesto, cream and 2 tablespoons of the basil in a bowl and mix until smooth. Season with salt and pepper. Mix in the remaining beaten egg. Spread the cheese mixture evenly over the pastry crust. Arrange the onions in a fan-shape bottom side up over the cheese layer.

Bake at 350 degrees for 20 minutes or until the crust is brown and the cheese is set. Cool on a wire rack. Sprinkle with the remaining 1 tablespoon basil. Cut into squares to serve. Yield: 18 servings.

Wine and Cheese Pairings

Cheese	Wine
Roquefort	Beaujolais
Gorgonzola	Cabernet Sauvignon
Brie	Alsace Riesling, Bordeaux
Camembert	Merlot
Appenzeller	Beaujolais
Cheddars	Beaujolais Nouveau, Cabernet Sauvignon, or Tawny Port
Fontina	Chianti Classico
Muenster	Alsace Riesling
Gouda	Red Rhone or Riesling
Parmesan	Vino Nobile, Barolo, Chianti Classico
Aged Goat Cheese	Sancerre
Bucheron	Chardonnay

Spinach Quenelles

2 (10-ounce) packages
  frozen spinach
2¹/₂ to 3 cups herb-
  seasoned stuffing
4 eggs, beaten
³/₄ cup margarine, softened
¹/₂ cup grated Parmesan
  cheese
1 onion, chopped
1 garlic clove, minced
¹/₂ teaspoon pepper

Thaw the spinach and drain well. Combine the spinach, stuffing, beaten eggs and margarine in a bowl and mix until well blended. Add the cheese, onion, garlic and pepper and mix well. Shape into 1-inch balls and place in a baking dish.

Bake at 350 degrees for 20 minutes. You may prepare the quenelles ahead and freeze before baking. Yield: 36 to 48 servings.

Spicy Sausage Bites

2 pounds spicy sausage
1 egg, lightly beaten
1/2 cup seasoned bread crumbs
1/2 teaspoon sage
1/2 cup ketchup
1/4 cup chili sauce
2 tablespoons brown sugar
1 tablespoon vinegar
1 tablespoon soy sauce

Combine the sausage, beaten egg, bread crumbs and sage in a large bowl and mix until well blended. Shape into 48 balls. Brown the sausage balls in a large skillet over high heat. Remove from heat and drain.

Combine the ketchup, chili sauce, brown sugar, vinegar and soy sauce in a bowl and mix well. Pour over the sausage balls.

Simmer, covered, over medium heat for 30 minutes. You may also place in a covered baking dish and bake at 350 degrees for 20 minutes. Serve warm. Yield: 48 servings.

Tortilla Wraps

1 (10-count) package large flour tortillas
6 ounces thinly sliced mozzarella cheese
1 cup roasted red peppers, drained
1 (8-ounce) tube sun-dried tomato spread
1 bunch fresh basil, chopped

Steam the tortillas for 30 to 60 seconds to soften. Slice the mozzarella cheese and peppers into thin strips.

Spread some of the sun-dried tomato spread on each tortilla. Layer with the mozzarella cheese, peppers and basil. Roll up tightly. Wrap the tortillas individually in aluminum foil.

Chill for at least 2 hours. Slice into 1-inch slices. Place a wooden pick in each slice and arrange on a serving plate. Yield: 50 servings.

Bar Setup

Set up your bar in the room where you want people to congregate. Always have appetizers or snacks to serve with your drinks. Use real glasses instead of plastic when possible; they always look much more elegant! If you allocate space for mixed drinks and a separate area for wine, it will alleviate congestion. It always adds to the fun to have a theme drink such as mint juleps, sangria, or margaritas.

Crab Meat Martini

7 scallions
1/2 cup pepper vodka
1/2 teaspoon dry vermouth
1 teaspoon lemon juice
Grated zest of 1 lemon
2 tablespoons lemon juice
Pepper
1 bunch watercress
8 ounces lump crab meat,
   rinsed

Freeze 4 martini glasses for at least 30 minutes. Slice 3 of the scallions, discarding the green tops. Combine the sliced scallions, pepper vodka, vermouth, 1 teaspoon lemon juice and lemon zest in a bowl and mix well. Moisten the rims of the martini glasses in 2 tablespoons lemon juice. Dip the moistened rims in pepper on a plate.

Place equal portions of the watercress in the bottom of the prepared glasses. Place 2 ounces of crab meat on top of the watercress in each glass. Pour the vodka mixture evenly into each prepared glass. Garnish with the remaining 4 scallions. Serve immediately. Yield: 4 servings.

Creamed Mussels with Whiskey and Wine

3/4 cup dry white wine
3/4 cup Irish whiskey
1 medium onion, finely
   chopped
3 pounds mussels,
   scrubbed and debearded
3/4 cup heavy cream
3 tablespoons fresh
   tarragon, minced

Combine the wine, whiskey and onion in a large saucepan. Add the mussels. Cook, covered, over high heat for 5 minutes or until the shells open. Discard any mussels that do not open. Add the cream and tarragon and bring to a simmer. Place the mussels in 6 serving bowls. Pour the cream sauce over the mussels and serve immediately. Yield: 6 servings.

Spicy Shrimp

½ cup olive oil
2 tablespoons Cajun seasoning
2 tablespoons lemon juice
2 tablespoons chopped parsley
1 tablespoon honey
1 tablespoon soy sauce
⅛ teaspoon cayenne pepper
1 pound shrimp, peeled, deveined

Combine the olive oil, Cajun seasoning, lemon juice, parsley, honey, soy sauce and cayenne pepper in a bowl. Add the shrimp and toss to coat well. Place in a baking dish and chill, covered, for 1 hour.

Bake at 450 degrees for 10 minutes or until the shrimp turn pink. Yield: 6 to 8 servings.

Cranberry Martinis

For Cranberry Martinis, rub 2 martini glass rims with a lime wedge and dip in 1 tablespoon red sanding sugar. Place the glasses in the freezer for 10 minutes or fill with ice. Skewer 5 whole cranberries on each of 2 wooden picks and set aside. Combine 8 ounces vodka, 1 ounce cranberry juice and 1 teaspoon vermouth in a cocktail shaker filled with ice and shake well. Strain the martini mixture into the chilled glasses and garnish with the cranberry skewers.

Tangy Apricot and Pineapple Grilling Sauce

1 (29-ounce) can tomato sauce
1 (12-ounce) jar apricot preserves
1 cup balsamic vinegar
1 cup white wine vinegar
1 (10-ounce) can crushed pineapple
1/2 cup packed brown sugar
1/2 cup sugar
1/4 cup teriyaki sauce
2 tablespoons soy sauce
2 tablespoons honey
2 tablespoons Worcestershire sauce
1 teaspoon onion powder
1 teaspoon garlic powder
1/2 to 1 teaspoon chili powder
2 tablespoons cornstarch
2 tablespoons water

Combine the tomato sauce, apricot preserves, balsamic vinegar, white wine vinegar, pineapple, brown sugar, sugar, teriyaki sauce, soy sauce, honey, Worcestershire sauce, onion powder, garlic powder and chili powder in a large saucepan. Bring to a boil over medium heat. Reduce the heat and simmer for 30 minutes. Combine the cornstarch and water in a bowl and mix until smooth. Stir into the sauce and simmer for 15 minutes. May be used as a baste for grilling chicken, beef or seafood. May also be used for meatballs, chicken kabobs and other appetizers. Yield: 5 cups

Football Punch

3 cups sugar
2 quarts sparkling water
2 quarts claret or cabernet
 sauvignon
1 pint brandy
1 pint rum
1 pint sparkling white wine
3/4 cup Italian vermouth

Combine the sugar, sparkling water, claret, brandy, rum, sparkling white wine and vermouth in a large punch bowl and mix well. Add a large ice ring and serve immediately. Yield: 24 to 36 servings.

Indian Summer Sangria

1 (750-milliliter) bottle
 beaujolais
1/4 cup orange liqueur
1/4 cup orange juice
2 tablespoons brandy
2 tablespoons sugar
6 to 8 orange slices
6 to 8 lemon slices
1 liter sparkling water

Combine the beaujolais, orange liqueur, orange juice, brandy and sugar in a large sealable container and mix well. Add the orange and lemon slices. Chill, covered, for 4 to 6 hours. Stir in the sparkling water immediately before serving. Serve over ice in glasses. Yield: 8 to 10 servings.

THE WELLER CENTER FOR HEALTH EDUCATION

*I*n 1981, the JLLV helped found the Weller Center for Health Education to perpetuate and share our commitment to physical and emotional wellness. Permanent and traveling exhibits teach children about the miraculous machine we call the human body— how it works, how it ages, and how to take care of it.

Now a freestanding, fully operational facility, the Weller Center remains one of the JLLV's most significant contributions to the Lehigh Valley.

Soups to Savor &
GREENS TO ENVY

Cold Cucumber Soup

3 cucumbers, peeled, seeded
1/2 cup finely chopped onion
3 cups chicken broth
1 cup sour cream
1 tablespoon finely chopped fresh parsley
1 teaspoon chopped fresh dill, or 1/4 teaspoon
     dried dill
Salt and pepper to taste

Coarsely chop 2 of the cucumbers. Combine the chopped
cucumbers, onion and chicken broth in a saucepan.
Simmer, covered, for 20 minutes.

Process the mixture 1/3 at a time in a blender until
smooth. Pour the mixture into a bowl. Grate the remaining
cucumber into the prepared mixture. Stir in the sour
cream, parsley and dill. Season with salt and pepper
and mix well.

Chill, covered, for 8 to 10 hours. Ladle into soup bowls.
Sprinkle with paprika if desired. Yield: 4 to 6 servings.

Gazpacho

1/3 loaf dried Italian bread
1 cup water
5 large ripe tomatoes, peeled, chopped
2 large cucumbers, peeled, chopped
1 large onion, chopped
1 large green bell pepper, chopped
5 large garlic cloves, chopped
3/4 cup red wine
2 tablespoons olive oil
2 teaspoons salt

Soak the bread in the water in a bowl for 1 to 2 minutes. Remove the crusts. Process the tomatoes, cucumbers, onion, bell pepper, garlic, red wine, olive oil, bread and salt 1/2 at a time in a blender until smooth. Pour into a large bowl.

Chill, covered, for 24 hours. Ladle into bowls. Garnish with chopped hard-cooked egg, onion, cucumber, green bell pepper and croutons. Yield: 4 to 6 servings.

Going to a Party

People appreciate and remember creative host or hostess gifts. Instead of wine or flowers, offer:

- An appetizer or dessert, arranged on a pretty new platter that the hostess gets to keep.

- A small herb garden in a terra-cotta planter.

- Gourmet coffee and homemade muffins for the next morning.

- A pretty picture frame.

- Aromatherapy candles.

- A Junior League cookbook!

Carrot and Orange Soup

This recipe is from Runaway Hill on Harbour
Island, Bahamas.

1/4 cup (1/2 stick) butter
2 cups finely chopped onions
12 large carrots, peeled and chopped
4 cups chicken broth
1 cup orange juice
Pinch of grated orange zest
Salt and pepper to taste

Melt the butter in a saucepan over low heat. Add the
onions and sauté for 25 minutes or until tender. Add the
carrots and chicken broth. Simmer for 30 minutes or until
the carrots are tender. Drain and reserve the broth.

Process the carrots and onions in a food processor until
smooth. Return to the saucepan with the reserved broth
and orange juice. Cook until heated through. Stir in the
orange zest, salt and pepper. Ladle into bowls to serve.
Yield: 6 servings.

Mushroom Onion Soup

1 tablespoon butter
1 tablespoon olive oil
2 onions, thinly sliced
1 garlic clove, minced
1 pound mushrooms, sliced
1 (6-ounce) can tomato paste
1 (46-ounce) can chicken broth
1/3 cup sweet vermouth
1 teaspoon salt
1/4 teaspoon pepper
2 tablespoons cornstarch
2 tablespoons water
2 tablespoons chopped fresh parsley

Heat the butter and olive oil in a large saucepan over medium heat. Add the onions and garlic and sauté until tender; do not brown Add the mushrooms and sauté for 3 minutes.

Stir in the tomato paste. Add the chicken broth and vermouth gradually, mixing well after each addition. Season with the salt and pepper and simmer for 1 minute.

Blend the cornstarch and water in a small bowl to make a paste. Add to the soup and mix well. Cook until thickened, stirring constantly. Add the parsley. Simmer for 30 to 45 minutes. Ladle into bowls to serve.
Yield: 8 servings.

"Ice" Bucket

Instead of using an ice bucket, place an empty wine bottle in an empty juice carton. Fill carton with water to just below the shoulder of the bottle. Freeze slightly and then drop in seasonal flowers or herbs (pansies, lavender, rosemary, mums, holly). Freeze until solid. Remove block of ice and bottle from carton. Thaw slightly and remove empty bottle. In its place, insert favorite wine or vodka.

Potato Leek Soup

4 or 5 large unpeeled red
    potatoes, coarsely
    chopped
3 cups chopped leeks
1 rib celery, chopped
1 large carrot, chopped
1/4 cup (1/2 stick) butter
3/4 teaspoon salt
1/2 cup water
3 cups milk
Salt and freshly ground
    pepper to taste

Combine the potatoes, leeks, celery, carrot, butter and 3/4 teaspoon salt in a saucepan. Cook over medium heat for 5 minutes. Add the water and bring to a boil. Reduce the heat. Simmer, covered, for 20 to 30 minutes or until the potatoes are tender, adding more water if needed. Remove from heat.

Combine the vegetable mixture with the milk in a blender container and process until smooth. Season with salt and pepper to taste. Return to the saucepan. Cook over medium heat until heated through; do not boil. Ladle into bowls to serve. You may prepare the soup 1 day in advance. May add additional milk when reheating. Do not use skim milk in this recipe. Yield: 6 to 8 servings.

Red Pepper Soup

3 red bell peppers
1 medium onion
1 large or 2 medium
    potatoes, peeled
2 tablespoons vegetable oil
1 garlic clove, minced
3 cups chicken broth
Salt and pepper to taste

Cut the bell peppers, onion and potatoes into thin slices. Heat the oil in a large saucepan over medium heat. Sauté the bell peppers, onion, potatoes and garlic in the oil until tender. Stir in the chicken broth. Simmer for 1 hour.

Pour the mixture into a blender container and process until smooth. Season with salt and pepper. Return to the saucepan and cook until heated through. Garnish with crème fraîche and/or miniature croutons. Ladle into bowls to serve. Yield: 4 to 6 servings.

Roasted Butternut Squash Bisque

Bisque

3 large butternut squash
4 sweet potatoes
5 onions, peeled, cut into
    quarters
3 carrots, coarsely chopped
4 ribs celery, coarsely
    chopped
3 garlic cloves, minced
6 tablespoons (3/4 stick)
    butter
1/2 teaspoon garlic powder
1/2 teaspoon cinnamon
3 pinches of nutmeg
6 cups water
4 tablespoons honey
1/2 cup heavy cream
Salt and pepper to taste

Maple Crème Fraîche

2 cups crème fraîche
2 tablespoons maple syrup

For the bisque, cut each squash into halves and remove the seeds. Place the squash on a greased baking sheet cut side down with the sweet potatoes and onions. Bake at 375 degrees for 20 minutes or until the vegetables are tender. Let cool.

Sauté the carrots, celery and garlic in the butter in a large saucepan for 3 minutes. Stir in the garlic powder, cinnamon and nutmeg. Add the water and simmer for 1 hour or longer. Peel and coarsely chop the squash and sweet potatoes. Add the squash, sweet potatoes and onions to the soup. Stir in the honey, cream, salt and pepper.

Process the soup in a blender until smooth. Return to the saucepan and season again if desired. Cook until heated through. Ladle into bowls to serve. Top with the Maple Crème Fraîche or sour cream. Yield: 6 to 8 servings.

For the Maple Crème Fraîche, combine the crème fraîche and maple syrup in a bowl and mix until well blended. Chill, covered, for 30 minutes or longer before serving.

Gypsy Vegetable Soup

3 to 4 tablespoons olive oil
2 cups chopped onions
2 cups chopped peeled sweet potatoes
1/2 cup chopped celery
2 garlic cloves, minced
3 cups water
2 teaspoons paprika
1 teaspoon basil
1 teaspoon turmeric
Dash of cinnamon
Dash of cayenne pepper
1 bay leaf
1 (15-ounce) can chick-peas
1 (14-ounce) can whole tomatoes, puréed
1 cup frozen green peas
1 tablespoon soy sauce
1 teaspoon salt

Heat the olive oil in a small kettle or Dutch oven over medium heat. Sauté the onions, sweet potatoes, celery and garlic in the olive oil for 5 minutes. Add the water, paprika, basil, turmeric, cinnamon, cayenne pepper and bay leaf. Simmer, covered, for 15 minutes.

Add the chick-peas, tomatoes and peas and simmer for 10 minutes or until the vegetables are tender. Add the soy sauce and salt and mix well. Remove the bay leaf. Ladle into bowls to serve. Yield: 6 to 8 servings.

Pasta Fagioli

1 cup olive oil
8 ounces pancetta, diced
4 ounces prosciutto, diced
4 links of hot Italian sausage, chopped
8 garlic cloves, minced
¼ teaspoon crushed red pepper flakes
¼ teaspoon black pepper
¼ teaspoon oregano
1 (16-ounce) can crushed tomatoes
1 cup sherry
3 cups chicken broth
8 cups cannellini
4 cups cooked ditalini pasta
1 cup grated Romano cheese

Heat the olive oil in a large saucepan or Dutch oven. Sauté the pancetta, prosciutto, sausage, garlic, red pepper flakes, black pepper and oregano in the olive oil until the meat is browned. Add the tomatoes and sherry and simmer for a few minutes. Add the chicken broth, beans and pasta and mix well. Cook until heated through. Top with the cheese. Ladle into bowls to serve.

Only add enough of the pasta for how many you are serving at one time. The pasta will not keep well in the soup because it will absorb the water and become mushy. Yield: 8 servings.

Skimming the Stock

Fold a paper towel in half, or use two, and pass it through the stock while it is still hot. Any fat will be quickly absorbed.

Cranberry Apple Salad

1 large thin-skinned orange, peeled
1 large red apple
2 cups fresh cranberries
1½ cups sugar
1 (3-ounce) package lemon gelatin
1 cup chopped celery
½ cup chopped walnuts

Cut the orange and apple into quarters. Remove the seeds and membranes from the orange. Process the orange, apple and cranberries in a food processor until finely chopped. Stir in the sugar until well blended.

Prepare the gelatin according to the package directions. Chill, covered, until partially set.

Fold in the cranberry mixture, celery and walnuts. Pour into a salad mold. Chill, covered, until set. This makes a great holiday salad. Yield: 8 to 10 servings.

Rich and Charlie's Salad

This recipe is from Rich and Charlie's, a famous Italian restaurant in St. Louis.

Parmesan Vinaigrette
1 cup salad oil
1/4 cup lemon juice
1/4 cup red wine vinegar
2 tablespoons sugar
2 teaspoons salt
1 teaspoon dry mustard
1/2 teaspoon garlic powder
1/2 teaspoon pepper
6 tablespoons grated
  Parmesan cheese

For the vinaigrette, combine the oil, lemon juice and red wine vinegar in a bowl and mix well. Whisk in the sugar, salt, dry mustard, garlic powder and pepper. Pour the vinaigrette into a jar with a tight-fitting lid. Add the cheese. Cover the jar and shake well to blend.

Salad
1 head iceberg lettuce
1 head romaine
1 (10-ounce) can artichoke
  hearts, chopped
1 (10-ounce) can hearts of
  palm, chopped
5 ounces roasted red peppers
1 large red onion, chopped

For the salad, chop the iceberg lettuce and romaine into bite-size pieces. Combine the lettuce, artichoke hearts, hearts of palm, red peppers and onion in a large salad bowl. Pour the vinaigrette over the salad and toss well before serving. Yield: 10 to 12 servings.

League Board Party Salad

Poppy Seed Vinaigrette

1 cup olive oil
1/2 cup red wine vinegar
1/2 cup sugar
1/3 cup finely chopped
    onion
1 teaspoon dry mustard
1 teaspoon paprika
1 teaspoon poppy seeds
1 teaspoon salt

For the vinaigrette, whisk the olive oil, red wine vinegar, sugar and onion in a bowl until well blended. Whisk in the dry mustard, paprika, poppy seeds and salt.

Almond Brittle

1/2 cup sugar
1/2 cup sliced almonds

For the brittle, melt the sugar in a saucepan over low heat, stirring constantly. Stir in the almonds until well coated. Pour onto a buttered plate. Let cool until hard. Break into small pieces.

Salad

1 head iceberg lettuce
1 head romaine
1 (8-ounce) can mandarin
    oranges
1/2 cup grapes
1/2 cup sliced strawberries
1/2 cups seasoned croutons
3 tablespoons grated
    Parmesan cheese

For the salad, chop the iceberg lettuce and romaine into bite-size pieces. Combine the lettuce, oranges, grapes, strawberries, croutons and cheese in a large salad bowl and toss well. Pour the vinaigrette over the salad and toss well to coat. Sprinkle the brittle on top of the salad.
Yield: 8 to 10 servings.

Red Leaf Lettuce with Raspberry Vinaigrette

Raspberry Vinaigrette
1/2 cup salad oil
3 tablespoons sugar
*3 tablespoons raspberry
    vinegar*
1 tablespoon lemon juice
1 tablespoon sour cream
*1 tablespoon Dijon
    mustard*
1 tablespoon poppy seeds
Salt and pepper to taste

For the vinaigrette, whisk the oil, sugar, raspberry vinegar, lemon juice, sour cream, Dijon mustard, poppy seeds, salt and pepper in a small bowl. Pour into a jar with a tight-fitting lid. Cover the jar and shake well to blend before serving.

Salad
1 head red leaf lettuce
2 cups fresh raspberries
*3/4 cup finely chopped red
    onion*
1/2 cup toasted walnuts

For the salad, chop the lettuce into bite-size pieces. Combine the lettuce, raspberries, onion and walnuts in a large bowl. Pour the vinaigrette over the salad and toss well before serving.
Yield: 6 to 8 servings.

Strawberry Spinach Salad

Cider Vinaigrette
1/2 cup sugar
1/4 cup apple cider vinegar
1 1/2 teaspoons minced
    dried onion
1/4 teaspoon paprika
1/4 teaspoon Worcestershire
    sauce
1/2 cup vegetable oil
1 tablespoon poppy seeds
1 tablespoon sesame seeds

Salad
10 ounces torn fresh
    spinach
1 1/2 cups sliced
    strawberries
1 small red onion, chopped
    (optional)
2 ounces bean sprouts
    (optional)

For the vinaigrette, combine the sugar, vinegar, dried onion, paprika and Worcestershire sauce in a blender container and process until well blended. Add the oil in a fine stream, processing constantly until smooth. Stir in the poppy seeds and sesame seeds.

For the salad, arrange the spinach on individual salad plates. Spoon the vinaigrette onto the spinach and top with the strawberries, onion and bean sprouts. Yield: 8 to 10 servings.

Spinach Medley and Red Wine Vinaigrette

Red Wine Vinaigrette
3/4 cup red wine vinegar
1/4 cup olive oil
2 teaspoons brown sugar
1 teaspoon garlic salt
1/2 teaspoon poppy seeds

Salad
1 red apple
Orange juice
1 1/2 pounds mixed
    spinach and leaf
    lettuce
1 (11-ounce) can
    mandarin oranges,
    drained
1 (8-ounce) package
    chopped sugared dates
    (see Note)
1 cup toasted pecans
3/4 cup sliced red onion

For the vinaigrette, combine the vinegar, olive oil, brown sugar, garlic salt and poppy seeds in a blender container and process until well blended.

For the salad, finely chop the apple and place in a bowl with a small amount of orange juice. Combine the spinach, lettuce, mandarin oranges, dates, pecans, apple and red onion in a large salad bowl and toss well. Serve the salad with the vinaigrette on the side. Yield: 8 servings.

Note: Most packages of chopped dates contain sugar, if not or chopping whole dates, add a small amount of sugar.

Lemon Coleslaw

Lemon Dressing

1/2 cup mayonnaise
1/2 cup sour cream
1/4 cup lemon juice
2 tablespoons Dijon
 mustard
2 tablespoons olive oil
2 tablespoons sugar
1 tablespoon white wine
 vinegar
1 tablespoon horseradish
2 teaspoons grated
 lemon zest
1 teaspoon salt
1/2 teaspoon celery seeds
1/2 teaspoon pepper

For the dressing, combine the mayonnaise, sour cream, lemon juice, Dijon mustard, olive oil, sugar, white wine vinegar, horseradish, lemon zest, salt, celery seeds and pepper in a bowl and whisk until well blended. Chill, covered, until serving time. You may prepare the dressing 1 day in advance.

Salad

8 cups shredded cabbage
2 carrots, grated
1/2 red or yellow bell
 pepper, thinly sliced
1/2 green bell pepper,
 thinly sliced
1/4 red onion, thinly sliced
2 tablespoons chopped
 fresh parsley

For the salad, combine the cabbage, carrots, red bell pepper, green bell pepper, onion and parsley in a large bowl. Toss with the dressing.
Yield: 10 to 12 servings.

Red Cabbage and Mango Salad

Cilantro Dressing
$1/3$ cup olive oil
$1/4$ cup rice vinegar
3 tablespoons sesame oil
2 tablespoons finely
    chopped fresh cilantro
$1/2$ teaspoon sugar
Salt and freshly ground
    pepper

For the dressing, whisk the olive oil, rice vinegar, sesame oil, cilantro, sugar, salt and pepper in a bowl until well blended.

Salad
2 ripe mangoes
2 small heads red cabbage,
    shredded
3 large tomatoes, sliced

For the salad, dice $2/3$ of the mangoes into small cubes and $1/3$ into large cubes. Toss the small mango cubes and cabbage with the dressing in a large bowl. Arrange the tomato slices in a circle in the center of the salad. Arrange the large mango cubes around the edge of the salad. Serve immediately. Yield: 4 to 6 servings.

Corn and Pea Salad

Dressing
3/4 cup sugar
3/4 cup vinegar
1/2 cup vegetable oil
1 teaspoon seasoned salt
1 teaspoon seasoned pepper

Salad
2 cups frozen baby green
*   peas, thawed*
2 cups frozen white corn,
*   thawed*
1 cup frozen green beans
1 cup chopped celery
1 cup chopped green bell
*   pepper*
1 bunch scallions, chopped
1 (2-ounce) jar pimentos

For the dressing, combine the sugar, vinegar, oil, salt and pepper in a medium saucepan. Bring to a boil, reduce the heat and cook for 10 minutes. Let cool.

For the salad, combine the peas, corn, green beans, celery, bell pepper, scallions and pimentos in a bowl and mix well. Pour the dressing over the salad and mix until well coated. Chill, covered, for at least 1 hour before serving. Yield: 8 servings.

Crab Meat Potato Salad with Warm Saffron Dressing

2 cups chicken broth
1 pound red potatoes, quartered
1/4 teaspoon saffron
3 tablespoons olive oil
1/2 cup chopped green onions
1/2 cup finely chopped red bell pepper
2 tablespoons minced garlic
2 tablespoons chopped fresh parsley
2 teaspoons salt
2 teaspoons freshly ground pepper
3 tablespoons olive oil
4 cups mixed greens
1/2 pound lump crab meat, cooked

Combine the broth, potatoes and saffron in a large saucepan. Bring to a boil over high heat and cook for 15 minutes or until the potatoes are tender. Remove from heat and let potatoes sit in the liquid for 10 minutes. Drain and reserve 1 cup liquid. Heat 3 tablespoons olive oil in a small saucepan over high heat. Sauté the green onions, bell pepper, garlic, parsley, salt and pepper for 30 seconds. Stir in the reserved liquid and bring to a simmer. Add the remaining 3 tablespoons olive oil, whisking until well blended and remove from heat.

To serve, arrange 1 cup mixed greens on each salad plate and top with 1/4 cup of the crab meat. Arrange the potatoes around the salad and spoon 5 to 6 tablespoons dressing over each salad. Serve immediately. This salad should be served warm. Yield: 4 to 6 servings.

New Potato Salad with Bacon and Mustard Seeds

2 tablespoons mustard seeds
1/3 cup balsamic vinegar
12 ounces thick-slice bacon, chopped
3 1/2 pounds small new potatoes
1 tablespoon plus 1/2 teaspoon salt
1/2 cup olive oil
1/2 cup chopped fresh parsley
2 teaspoons pepper

Soak the mustard seeds in the vinegar in a small bowl for 1 hour. Cook the bacon in a large heavy skillet over medium heat for 8 minutes or until crisp, stirring occasionally. Remove the bacon to paper towels to drain.

Combine the potatoes with enough water to cover in a large saucepan. Add 1 tablespoon of the salt. Bring to a boil and cook for 20 minutes or until the potatoes are tender. Drain and let cool slightly. Cut the potatoes into quarters and place in a large bowl.

Stir the remaining 1/2 teaspoon salt into the vinegar mixture. Pour over the potatoes and toss to coat. Let cool to room temperature. Add the bacon, olive oil, parsley and pepper to the potatoes and mix well, adding more vinegar if desired. You may prepare the salad 6 hours in advance and chill, covered, in the refrigerator. Serve at room temperature. Yield: 10 servings.

Primavera Salad

4 fresh asparagus stalks
1 or 2 zucchini
1/2 pound spaghetti
1/2 cup fresh or thawed frozen green peas,
*   cooked tender-crisp*
1 cup chopped broccoli florets, cooked tender-crisp
1/4 pound mushrooms, sliced
2 cups chopped tomatoes
3 tablespoons chopped basil
1/4 cup chopped fresh parsley
1 1/2 cups mayonnaise
2 tablespoons minced garlic
2 tablespoons white vinegar
Salt and pepper to taste
1/2 cup toasted pine nuts

Trim the asparagus and peel the ends. Cut diagonally into 1-inch pieces. Cook in enough water to cover in a saucepan until tender-crisp. Drain and set aside. Slice the zucchini lengthwise into 4 quarters. Cut each quarter into 1/2-inch pieces. Cook in enough water to cover in a saucepan until tender-crisp. Drain and set aside. Break the spaghetti into halves. Cook in enough water to cover for 7 minutes or until tender; drain. Rinse and drain.

Combine the asparagus, zucchini, peas, broccoli and spaghetti in a large bowl. Add the mushrooms, tomatoes, basil and parsley and mix well. Combine the mayonnaise, garlic and vinegar in a small bowl and mix until well blended. Add to the salad and toss to coat. Season with salt and pepper. Sprinkle with the pine nuts. Serve at room temperature. Yield: 8 to 10 servings.

Edible Flowers for Garnishing

Roses, Petunias, Pansies, Johnny-jump-ups, Violets, Primrose, Pot Marigold, Calendula, Day Lily (Yellow or Orange only), Impatiens, Lavender, Sweet Basil, Nasturtiums, Tulips (remove center), Borage, Sweet William, Hollyhock (Remember that everything you place on your plate should be edible. Also, do not use flowers that have been sprayed with pesticides.)

Tomato, Basil and Couscous Salad

2¹/₄ cups chicken broth
1 (10-ounce) package couscous
1 cup chopped green onions
1 cup chopped seeded tomatoes
¹/₃ cup thinly sliced fresh basil
¹/₂ cup olive oil
¹/₄ cup balsamic vinegar
¹/₄ teaspoon dried crushed red pepper
Salt and black pepper to taste
Cherry tomatoes or grape tomatoes, halved

Bring the chicken broth to a boil in a saucepan. Add the couscous. Remove from heat and let stand, covered, for 5 minutes.

Remove to a large bowl and fluff with a fork. Let cool. Add the green onions, chopped tomatoes, basil, olive oil, vinegar and red pepper and mix well. Season with salt and black pepper.

You may prepare 1 day in advance and chill, covered, in the refrigerator. Top with cherry tomatoes before serving. Yield: 6 to 8 servings.

Confetti Rice Salad

Dijon Vinaigrette
$^1/_2$ *cup olive oil*
$^1/_4$ *cup red wine vinegar*
1 tablespoon Dijon
*   mustard*
1 teaspoon sugar
$^1/_2$ *teaspoon salt*
$^1/_2$ *teaspoon pepper*
Chives to taste

For the vinaigrette, combine the olive oil, vinegar, Dijon mustard, sugar, salt, pepper and chives in a blender container and process until well blended.

Salad
$2^1/_2$ *cups rice*
$^1/_2$ *green bell pepper,*
*   chopped*
$^1/_2$ *red bell pepper, chopped*
6 scallions, thinly sliced
$^1/_2$ *cup dried currants*
$^1/_4$ *cup chopped black olives*
1 to 2 teaspoons chopped
*   fresh dill*
1 teaspoon parsley

For the salad, cook the rice according to the package directions. Add 3/4 cup of the dressing to the hot rice. Let cool. Add the green bell pepper, red bell pepper, scallions, currants, black olives, dill and parsley and mix well. Add the remaining dressing if desired. Serve immediately. You may prepare the salad and chill, covered, 4 hours in advance. Bring to room temperature before serving. Yield: 6 servings.

THE DISCOVERY CENTER OF SCIENCE AND TECHNOLOGY

*O*riginally an educational science fair for children and their families, the Discovery Center of Science and Technology was born out of an innovative collaboration between the JLLV, the Junior Women's Club of Bethlehem, and Lehigh University.

Like other programs that the JLLV has helped nurture from infancy, the Discovery Center is now an independently operated hands-on learning center. Permanent and traveling exhibits help children explore the wonders of math, nature, communications, and more.

Sumptuous
SIDES

Marinated Asparagus

1 cup extra-virgin olive oil
1/3 cup red wine vinegar
1/3 cup chopped green bell pepper
2 tablespoons chopped pimentos
2 tablespoons chopped green onions
1 tablespoon chopped fresh parsley
1 tablespoon salt
1 teaspoon sugar
1 pound fresh thin asparagus,
    trimmed and blanched

Combine the olive oil, vinegar, bell pepper, pimentos, green onions, parsley, salt and sugar in a shallow nonmetallic bowl. Add the asparagus and toss to coat.

Marinate, covered, in the refrigerator for several hours. Serve chilled or at room temperature.
Yield: 4 to 6 servings.

Cuban Black Beans

1 pound dried black beans
1 large bell pepper, halved
10 cups water
2/3 cup olive oil
1 large onion, chopped
4 garlic cloves, minced
4 teaspoons salt
1/2 teaspoon pepper
1/4 teaspoon oregano
1 bay leaf
2 tablespoons sugar
2 tablespoons vinegar
2 tablespoons dry white wine
2 tablespoons olive oil

Sort and rinse the beans. Soak the beans and bell pepper in the water in a large pot for 8 to 10 hours. Remove the bell pepper. Chop the bell pepper finely and set aside. Bring the beans to a boil and cook for 45 minutes or until the beans are soft. Heat 2/3 cup olive oil in a skillet and sauté the onion, garlic and bell pepper until tender. Add 1 cup of the beans to the skillet and mash the beans well. Add the onion mixture to the large pot of beans. Stir in the salt, pepper, oregano, bay leaf and sugar.

Cook for 1 hour, stirring occasionally. Add the vinegar and wine and cook for 1 hour. Remove the bay leaf. Stir in 2 tablespoons olive oil immediately before serving. Serve over cooked white rice. Yield: 8 to 10 servings.

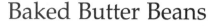

Baked Butter Beans

8 slices bacon, chopped
1 cup ketchup
1/2 cup packed brown sugar
1/3 cup dark corn syrup
1 tablespoon mustard
Salt and pepper to taste
4 (13-ounce) packages
  frozen butter beans

Cook the bacon in a skillet until crisp. Combine the ketchup, brown sugar, corn syrup, mustard, salt and pepper in a saucepan. Bring the mixture to a boil and remove from heat. Stir in the bacon and butter beans. Pour into a baking dish. Bake, covered, at 300 degrees for 2 hours. Remove the cover and bake for 30 minutes. Yield: 8 to 10 servings.

Asian String Beans

2 tablespoons peanut oil
2 tablespoons minced garlic
1 tablespoon fresh grated
  gingerroot
1 pound green beans,
  trimmed
1/4 teaspoon five-spice
  powder
1/4 cup soy sauce

Heat the peanut oil in a wok over high heat. Sauté the garlic and ginger for 1 or 2 minutes. Add the beans and five-spice powder and sauté for 5 minutes or until tender-crisp. Add the soy sauce and sauté for about 30 seconds. Serve immediately. Yield: 6 to 8 servings.

Green Bean and Onion Vinaigrette

¹/₂ pound fresh green beans
Salt to taste
1 tablespoon finely chopped parsley
2 teaspoons red wine vinegar
1 teaspoon Dijon mustard
3 tablespoons olive oil
Freshly ground pepper
12 thin red onion slices

Trim the beans. Bring enough salted water to cover to a boil in a saucepan. Add the beans and cook for 5 minutes or until tender-crisp. Drain and rinse the beans under cold water. Remove to a serving dish.

Combine the parsley, vinegar and mustard in a large bowl. Whisk in the olive oil, salt and pepper. Arrange the onion slices on top of the beans. Pour the vinaigrette over the beans and onion. Yield: 4 to 6 servings.

Setting the Table

Start your setting with dinner plates or larger decorative chargers. Arrange no more than three pieces of silverware on each side of the dinner plate. The service should be placed in order of the use for each course, beginning on the outside and working in. Forks go on the left, with knives and spoons on the right. Knives should be placed with the cutting edge toward the dinner plate, on the inside of the spoon(s). Place dessert forks and spoons above the dinner plate— spoon closest to the plate with handle facing right, and fork above it with handle facing left.

Braised Brussels Sprouts with Olive Oil and Garlic

20 medium-large brussels sprouts
$1/2$ cup water
2 tablespoons olive oil
1 teaspoon fresh thyme
$1/2$ teaspoon minced garlic

Trim the brussels sprouts. Combine with the water in a microwave-safe bowl. Microwave on High for 5 minutes. Remove the brussels sprouts and slice into halves, lengthwise.

Drizzle 1 tablespoon of the olive oil into a 9-inch baking dish. Arrange the brussels sprouts cut side up in the dish. Drizzle the remaining 1 tablespoon olive oil over the brussels sprouts. Sprinkle with the thyme and garlic.

Bake at 350 degrees for 30 to 40 minutes or until tender. Season as desired. Yield: 4 to 6 servings.

Gingered Carrot Purée

2 large potatoes, peeled, chopped
12 medium carrots, coarsely chopped
1/2 small onion, finely chopped
6 tablespoons (3/4 stick) butter
1 1/2 teaspoons ginger
1 tablespoon honey

Cook the potatoes in boiling water in a saucepan until tender. Cook the carrots in boiling water in a saucepan until tender. Drain and reserve the water.

Sauté the onion in 1 tablespoon of the butter until translucent. Combine the carrots and potatoes in a large bowl and mash with a handheld masher. Add the onion and remaining 5 tablespoons butter and beat with a hand mixer. Beat in enough of the reserved water to reach the desired consistency. Add the ginger and honey and mix well.

May substitute the desired amount of cream for the reserved water. Spoon the mixture into a pastry tube fitted with a decorator tip. Pipe into rosettes to serve. Yield: 6 servings.

How to Arrange the Glasses

Set glasses to the right, above the knife, beginning with a water goblet. Follow with a white wine glass, and then, if two wines are being served, with the red wine glass.

Harvest Corn Pudding

4 (13-ounce) cans whole
  kernel corn
1 cup half-and-half
6 eggs, beaten
$^1/_2$ cup (1 stick) butter,
  melted
$^1/_2$ cup flour
2 tablespoons sugar

Combine the corn and half-and-half in a large bowl. Whisk in the beaten eggs until well blended. Add the melted butter, flour and sugar and mix well. Pour into a greased 9×13 inch baking dish. Bake at 350 degrees for 45 minutes or until a knife inserted in the center comes out clean.
Yield: 8 to 10 servings.

Eggplant Casserole

3 medium eggplant, peeled
$1^1/_2$ tablespoons olive oil
1 (28-ounce) can peeled
  whole tomatoes
1 large onion, sliced
2 cups shredded sharp
  Cheddar cheese
Bread crumbs

Slice the eggplant into 1-inch slices. Cut the slices into 1-inch pieces. Sauté the eggplant in the olive oil in a skillet just until tender. Alternate layers of eggplant, tomatoes, onion and cheese in a 9-inch casserole sprayed with nonstick cooking spray, ending with a cheese layer. Top with bread crumbs.

Bake at 350 degrees for 30 to 45 minutes. Serve with warm crusty French bread. This casserole makes a wonderful vegetarian main dish.
Yield: 10 servings.

Greek Potatoes

6 medium potatoes, cubed
1/2 cup fresh lemon juice
1/3 cup vegetable oil
1 tablespoon olive oil
2 teaspoons salt
1/2 teaspoon pepper
1 1/2 teaspoons dried oregano
2 garlic cloves, minced
3 cups hot water

Combine the unpeeled potatoes, lemon juice, vegetable oil and olive oil in a large deep baking pan. Stir in the salt, pepper, oregano and garlic. Add the hot water.

Bake at 375 degrees for 1 1/2 hours or until the water evaporates and the potatoes are tender, stirring every 20 minutes and adding more water if needed. Be careful to not let the potatoes stick to the pan or burn.
Yield: 6 to 8 servings.

Worth Repeating

A colorful and dramatic centerpiece is a large quantity of one flower type. Cut the stems short and place flowers in glass punch bowls, individual glasses, bowls, or silver Jefferson cups and run them down the center of the table. (Placing a candle in between adds even more drama.)

Roquefort Potato Gratin

5 pounds russet potatoes, peeled
Salt and pepper to taste
2 cups heavy cream
5 ounces Roquefort cheese, crumbled
1/2 cup dried bread crumbs
1 1/2 tablespoons dried rosemary
1/4 cup (1/2 stick) butter, cut into small pieces

Cut the potatoes into 1/8-inch slices. Layer the potatoes in a buttered 10×15-inch baking dish, seasoning each layer with salt and pepper.

Bring the cream to a boil in a saucepan and reduce the heat to medium. Add the cheese to the cream. Cook until melted, whisking constantly. Pour over the potatoes.

Bake, covered with foil, at 425 degrees for 1 hour or until the potatoes are tender. Remove from the oven and preheat the broiler.

Combine the bread crumbs and rosemary in a small bowl. Sprinkle over the potatoes and dot with the butter. Broil for 4 minutes or until the bread crumbs are golden brown and the butter is melted. Let stand for 10 minutes before serving. Yield: 8 servings.

Savory Mashed Potatoes

4 pounds potatoes, peeled
8 ounces cream cheese
1 cup sour cream
1 garlic clove, minced
2 teaspoons salt
Dash of pepper
1/4 cup chopped chives
Paprika
Butter
1/2 cup grated Parmesan cheese (optional)

Combine the potatoes with enough water to cover in a saucepan. Bring to a boil. Boil until tender; drain. Mash the potatoes in a large mixing bowl. Add the cream cheese, sour cream, garlic, salt, pepper and chives. Beat at high speed until smooth.

Spread into a lightly greased baking dish. Sprinkle with the paprika and dot with the butter. Top with the Parmesan cheese. You may chill, covered, until ready to bake.

Bake at 350 degrees for 30 minutes or until heated through. Serve immediately. Yield: 6 to 8 servings.

Scalloped Potatoes with Leeks and Cream

1/4 cup (1/2 stick) unsalted butter
4 cups chopped leeks (white and pale
green parts only)
Salt and pepper to taste
1 tablespoon butter
2 cups heavy cream
3 garlic cloves, minced
3 pounds potatoes, peeled, thinly sliced
2 cups shredded white Cheddar cheese
1/3 cup grated Parmesan cheese

Melt 1/4 cup butter in a large heavy skillet over medium
heat. Add the leeks, stirring to coat. Reduce the heat.
Cook, covered, for 8 minutes or until the leeks are tender,
stirring occasionally. Cook, uncovered, for 3 minutes or
until almost all the liquid is absorbed. Season with salt
and pepper. Remove from heat. Grease a 9×13-inch
baking dish with 1 tablespoon butter. Combine the cream
and garlic in a small bowl. Arrange half the potatoes in
the prepared dish. Season with salt and pepper. Top
with the leeks, half the Cheddar cheese and half the
cream mixture. Layer with the remaining potatoes,
Cheddar cheese and cream mixture. Sprinkle with the
Parmesan cheese.

Bake at 375 degrees for 1 1/4 hours or until the potatoes
are tender and the top is golden brown. Let stand for
15 minutes before serving. You may prepare the dish up to
6 hours in advance. Chill, covered, until ready to bake.
Return to room temperature before baking.
Yield: 6 to 8 servings.

Sweet Potato Soufflé

2 large sweet potatoes, peeled and cooked
1/2 cup sugar
2 tablespoons butter
1/2 teaspoon salt
Pinch of nutmeg
1 teaspoon almond extract
1/4 cup heavy cream
1/2 cup dry sherry
3/4 cup chopped pecans
1 tablespoon butter

Place the sweet potatoes in a food processor container. Process until smooth. Add the sugar, 2 tablespoons butter, salt, nutmeg, almond extract, cream and sherry. Process until smooth.

Brown the pecans in 1 tablespoon butter in a small skillet. Stir the pecans into the sweet potato mixture.

Spoon into a soufflé dish or an 8×8-inch baking dish. Bake at 350 degrees for 30 minutes. Yield: 6 servings.

Butternut Squash Bake

1 butternut squash
1/4 cup (1/2 stick) butter
1 teaspoon cinnamon
1/4 to 1/2 teaspoon nutmeg
1/2 cup packed brown sugar
1/4 cup (1/2 stick) butter
1/2 cup chopped pecans
1/4 cup packed brown sugar
1 to 2 tart apples, peeled, thinly sliced

Cut the squash into halves lengthwise and scoop out the seeds. Place the squash on a baking sheet. Bake at 350 degrees for 40 to 60 minutes or until tender. Scoop the pulp into a bowl. Discard the peel. Mash the squash with a handheld masher. Add 1/4 cup butter, cinnamon, nutmeg and 1/2 cup brown sugar and mix well. Spoon into a 9-inch round baking pan.

Combine 1/4 cup butter, pecans and 1/4 cup brown sugar in a bowl and mix until crumbly. Sprinkle over the squash. Arrange the apple slices in a decorative circle over the top. Bake for 20 minutes or until the apples are tender and the squash is heated through. Yield: 4 servings.

New Orleans Spinach

2 (9-ounce) packages frozen chopped spinach
8 ounces cream cheese, softened
1/4 cup (1/2 stick) butter, softened
Zest of 1 lemon
Juice of 1/2 lemon
Pinch of nutmeg
Pinch of cayenne pepper
Salt to taste
1 cup stuffing mix or crushed croutons
1/4 cup (1/2 stick) butter, melted

Cook the spinach according to package directions; drain. Add the cream cheese and 1/4 cup butter and mix until well combined.

Add the lemon zest, lemon juice, nutmeg, cayenne pepper and salt and mix well. Spoon into a greased baking dish. Spread the stuffing mix on top. Drizzle with the melted butter. Bake at 350 degrees for 30 minutes. Yield: 6 to 8 servings.

Napkins

Use wire-edged ribbon instead of standard napkin rings to tie bows around your napkins. You can use seasonal colors and tie flowers or greens in for an extra touch.

Scalloped Tomatoes

1 (14-ounce) can crushed tomatoes
8 or 9 Lineda biscuits, crushed
$^1\!/_2$ teaspoon garlic powder
$^1\!/_4$ teaspoon sugar
$^1\!/_4$ teaspoon salt
$^1\!/_4$ teaspoon seasoned salt
$^1\!/_4$ teaspoon pepper
8 ounces sharp Cheddar cheese, sliced or shredded
2 tablespoons butter

Combine the undrained tomatoes, crushed biscuits, garlic powder, sugar, salt, seasoned salt and pepper in a large bowl and mix well. Spoon into a buttered 9×13-inch baking dish. Cover with the cheese. Dot with the butter.

Bake at 350 degrees for 40 minutes or until brown and bubbly. You may substitute crushed oyster crackers for the Lineda biscuits. Yield: 8 servings.

Seven-Vegetable Casserole

2 medium zucchini
1 large carrot, thinly sliced
1 rib celery
1/2 green bell pepper
1/2 red bell pepper
1 banana pepper, finely chopped
1 large tomato, peeled, chopped
1/2 small onion, coarsely chopped
1/2 cup chicken broth
3/4 cup shredded sharp Cheddar cheese
Salt to taste
3/4 cup shredded sharp Cheddar cheese

Cut the zucchini and celery crosswise into 1/4-inch slices. Cut the bell peppers into 1/2-inch pieces. Combine the zucchini, carrot, celery, bell peppers, banana pepper, tomato, onion, chicken broth and 3/4 cup cheese in a large bowl. Season with salt. Spoon into a 9-inch casserole.

Bake, covered, at 350 degrees for 1 to 1 1/2 hours or until the carrot is tender, topping with 3/4 cup cheese during the last 15 minutes of baking time. Serve in small individual bowls or drain with a slotted spoon to serve.

You may prepare the casserole up to 5 days in advance. Chill, covered, in the refrigerator. Return to room temperature before baking. Yield: 8 to 10 servings.

Oyster Stuffing

1 large onion
1 rib celery
1 cup (2 sticks) margarine
1 cup giblets
1 dozen fresh small stewing oysters, chopped
1 cup oyster liquor
2 (14-ounce) packages seasoned stuffing
4 slices dry bread, torn into pieces
1 tablespoon parsley
1 teaspoon sage
1 teaspoon marjoram
1 teaspoon thyme
2 teaspoons salt
1 teaspoon pepper

Chop the onion and celery in a food processor. Sauté
the onion and celery in the margarine in a large skillet
until transparent. Add the giblets to the skillet.

Combine the oysters and oyster liquor in a small
saucepan. Bring to a boil and cook for 3 to 5 minutes.
Add to the onion mixture.

Add the stuffing, dry bread, parsley, sage, marjoram,
thyme, salt and pepper. Simmer until the liquid is absorbed
but mixture is not dry. Yield: 10 servings.

Old South Sausage Stuffing

2 (8-ounce) packages corn bread stuffing mix
1 (8-ounce) package herb-seasoned stuffing mix
2 cups water
2 chicken bouillon cubes
1 cup (2 sticks) butter
½ cup chopped green bell pepper
½ cup chopped celery
¾ cup chopped onion
1 cup (2 sticks) butter
1 pound ground sausage
2 eggs, beaten
¾ cup chopped pecans
1 teaspoon marjoram
½ teaspoon pepper

Prepare the stuffing mixes according to the package directions using 2 cups water, bouillon cubes and 1 cup butter. Sauté the bell pepper, celery and onion in 1 cup butter in a large skillet until the bell pepper is tender and the celery and onion are transparent. Remove the bell pepper, celery and onion from the skillet. Brown the sausage in the skillet, stirring until crumbly.

Combine the prepared stuffing, bell pepper, celery, onion, sausage, eggs, pecans, marjoram and pepper in a large bowl and mix well. Spread over the bottom of a baking dish. Bake at 350 degrees for 30 minutes or until golden brown. Do not overcook. You may also use to stuff a 16- to 20-pound turkey. Yield: 12 to 14 servings.

TURNING POINT II

We believe that every person has the right to live in a home without violence. In 1986, we turned that belief into action through the acquisition and renovation of a second shelter for the domestic violence refuge, Turning Point.

Over the course of four years, the JLLV shepherded this project toward completion through valuable partnerships with other nonprofits, industry, and government agencies. The JLLV was recognized with the BMW Community Impact Merit Award in 1990. But the greatest reward is the knowledge that we helped to provide the women and children in our community with a safe place to rest their heads.

Divine
DINNERS

Look for our wine recommendations
at the end of each recipe!

Fillet of Beef

1 (3- to 4-pound) whole beef fillet, trimmed
2 teaspoons garlic slivers
Extra-virgin olive oil
Kitchen Bouquet
Sugar
1/2 cup red wine
1/2 cup beef bouillon

Line a baking pan with heavy-duty foil, allowing a 6-inch overhang. Bring the beef to room temperature. Make slits in the surface of the fillet. Sauté the garlic in olive oil in a skillet. Push the garlic slivers into the slits using the end of a sharp knife. Rub the surface of the beef with Kitchen Bouquet. Rub with a generous amount of olive oil and sprinkle with sugar. Place the beef in the prepared baking pan. Broil until seared on all sides, turning frequently. Remove from oven. Let stand until room temperature.

Add the red wine and bouillon to the baking pan. Seal the foil, leaving some airspace in the packet. Bake at 325 degrees for 20 to 25 minutes or until of the desired degree of doneness. Let stand until room temperature. Slice thinly and arrange on a serving platter. Serve with a cabernet sauvignon. Yield: 6 to 8 servings.

Rocky Mountain Grilled Flank Steak

Recipe from the Inn of the Falcon, Bethlehem

1 (1- to 2-pound) flank steak
2 cups olive oil
1/4 cup soy sauce
2 tablespoons Worcestershire sauce
2 tablespoons chopped fresh basil
1 tablespoon minced fresh marjoram
2 teaspoons minced fresh oregano
1 teaspoon minced fresh thyme
1 large garlic clove, minced
Freshly ground pepper to taste
1 small onion, thinly sliced

Place the steak in a shallow nonreactive dish. Combine the olive oil, soy sauce, Worcestershire sauce, basil, marjoram, oregano, thyme, garlic and pepper in a bowl and mix well. Pour over the steak, turning to coat. Marinate, covered, in the refrigerator for up to 24 hours, turning occasionally.

Prepare a charcoal fire; the coals are ready when they turn white. Soak 1/2 cup mesquite or other wood chips in water in a bowl for 20 to 30 minutes; drain. Place the chips over the hot coals just before placing the steak on the grill rack. Drain the steak, discarding the marinade. Place the steak on the grill rack. Grill for 10 minutes per side for rare or until of the desired degree of doneness. Slice the steak diagonally across the grain. Arrange the slices on a serving platter. Top with the onion. Serve with a zinfandel or rich cabernet sauvignon. Yield: 2 to 4 servings.

Strip Steak with Pale Ale and Shallot Sauce

1^1/$_2$ cups beef stock
^{3}/$_4$ cup pale ale (such as
    Bass), flat, at room
    temperature
4 tablespoons (^{1}/$_2$ stick)
    unsalted butter
6 (6- to 8-ounce) New York
    strip steaks, 1 inch thick
1 teaspoon thyme, crushed
Salt and pepper to taste
2 large shallots, minced
1 tablespoon brown sugar
1 tablespoon red wine
    vinegar
^{1}/$_4$ cup (^{1}/$_2$ stick) unsalted
    butter, chilled, sliced

Combine the stock and ale in a heavy saucepan and mix well. Bring to a boil. Boil for 8 minutes or until reduced to 1 cup, stirring frequently. Remove from heat. Heat 2 tablespoons butter in each of 2 large heavy skillets over medium-high heat. Sprinkle the steaks with thyme, salt and pepper. Add 3 steaks to each skillet. Cook for 4 minutes per side for medium-rare or until of the desired degree of doneness. Transfer the steaks to a platter with a slotted spoon. Cover with foil to keep warm.

Discard all but 1 tablespoon of the pan drippings from 1 skillet. Stir the shallots into the reserved pan drippings. Sauté for 2 minutes or until tender. Stir in the stock mixture, brown sugar and wine vinegar. Bring to a boil over high heat.

Boil for 4 minutes or until reduced to ^{2}/$_3$ cup, stirring frequently. Remove from heat. Add ^{1}/$_4$ cup butter gradually, whisking constantly until blended. Season with pepper. Ladle over the steaks. Serve immediately. Additional sauce may be served at the table. Serve with a hearty zinfandel.
Yield: 6 servings.

Rib-Tickling Baked Beef Stew

1 (14-ounce) can diced tomatoes
1 cup water
3 tablespoons quick-cooking tapioca
2 tablespoons sugar
1 teaspoon salt
1/2 teaspoon pepper
2 pounds lean beef stew meat, cut into 1-inch cubes
4 medium carrots, cut into 1-inch chunks
3 medium potatoes, peeled, cut into quarters
2 ribs celery, cut into 3/4-inch chunks
1 medium onion, sliced
1 slice bread, cubed

Combine the undrained tomatoes, water, tapioca, sugar, salt and pepper in a large bowl and mix well. Stir in the stew meat, carrots, potatoes, celery, onion and bread. Spoon into a greased 9×13-inch baking pan or 3-quart baking dish.

Bake, covered, at 375 degrees for 1 3/4 to 2 hours or until the beef and vegetables are of the desired degree of doneness. Serve with a merlot. Yield: 6 to 8 servings.

Chili

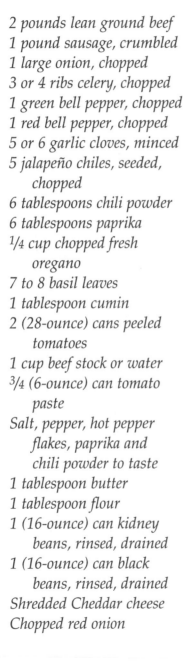

2 pounds lean ground beef
1 pound sausage, crumbled
1 large onion, chopped
3 or 4 ribs celery, chopped
1 green bell pepper, chopped
1 red bell pepper, chopped
5 or 6 garlic cloves, minced
5 jalapeño chiles, seeded,
    chopped
6 tablespoons chili powder
6 tablespoons paprika
1/4 cup chopped fresh
    oregano
7 to 8 basil leaves
1 tablespoon cumin
2 (28-ounce) cans peeled
    tomatoes
1 cup beef stock or water
3/4 (6-ounce) can tomato
    paste
Salt, pepper, hot pepper
    flakes, paprika and
    chili powder to taste
1 tablespoon butter
1 tablespoon flour
1 (16-ounce) can kidney
    beans, rinsed, drained
1 (16-ounce) can black
    beans, rinsed, drained
Shredded Cheddar cheese
Chopped red onion

Cook the ground beef and sausage in a skillet until gray in color; do not brown. Drain the ground beef mixture. Sauté the onion, celery, bell peppers, garlic and chiles in a nonstick skillet until tender. Combine the ground beef mixture and onion mixture in a large saucepan and mix well. Stir in 6 tablespoons chili powder, 6 tablespoons paprika, oregano, basil and cumin.

Cook over medium heat for 10 minutes or until the flavors are released, stirring occasionally. Crush the tomatoes and add the tomatoes and juice to the ground beef mixture. Stir in the stock. Simmer for 1 hour, stirring occasionally. Stir in the tomato paste. Simmer for 30 minutes, stirring occasionally. Add salt, pepper, hot pepper flakes, paprika and chili powder to taste. Simmer for 15 to 20 minutes, stirring occasionally.

Heat the butter in a saucepan until melted. Stir in the flour. Cook until bubbly, stirring constantly. Stir into the chili. Add the beans and mix well. Simmer for 10 to 15 minutes or until heated through and thickened. Ladle into chili bowls. Top with shredded cheese and chopped red onion. Serve with a Mexican beer. Yield: 10 to 12 servings.

Not-Your-Typical-Boring Meat Loaf

3 tablespoons unsalted
    butter
³/₄ cup finely chopped onion
³/₄ cup finely chopped
    scallions or green onion
    bulbs with tops
¹/₂ cup finely chopped carrot
¹/₄ cup minced red
    bell pepper
¹/₄ cup minced green
    bell pepper
2 teaspoons minced garlic
3 eggs, beaten
1 teaspoon freshly ground
    black pepper
1 teaspoon cumin
¹/₂ teaspoon ground white
    pepper
¹/₂ teaspoon freshly grated
    nutmeg
¹/₄ teaspoon cayenne pepper
Salt to taste
¹/₂ cup ketchup
¹/₂ cup half-and-half
2 pounds lean ground beef
    chuck, crumbled
12 ounces sausage,
    crumbled
¹/₄ cup fresh fine bread
    crumbs, toasted

Heat the butter in a heavy skillet until melted. Stir in the onion, scallions, carrot, bell peppers and garlic. Cook for 10 minutes or until the moisture from the vegetables has evaporated, stirring frequently. Let stand until cool. Chill, covered, for 1 hour or longer.

Combine the eggs, black pepper, cumin, white pepper, nutmeg, cayenne pepper and salt in a bowl and mix well. Stir in the ketchup and half-and-half. Add the ground chuck, sausage and bread crumbs and mix well. Stir in the chilled vegetable mixture.

Shape the ground chuck mixture into an oval loaf. Place the loaf in a baking dish. Place the baking dish in a larger baking pan. Add just enough boiling water to the baking pan to reach halfway up the sides of the baking dish. Bake at 375 degrees for 35 to 40 minutes or until cooked through. Remove the baking dish from the water bath. Let the meat loaf stand for 20 minutes before serving. Leftovers are even better. Serve with a cabernet sauvignon. Yield: 6 to 8 servings.

Lamb with Peppercorn Crust

1 (5-pound) leg of lamb, boned
1/2 cup dry red wine
1/2 cup raspberry vinegar
1/4 cup soy sauce
5 garlic cloves, crushed
1 1/2 teaspoons rosemary
2 tablespoons Dijon mustard
3 tablespoons mixed red, green, black and white
  peppercorns, crushed

Place the lamb flat in a shallow nonreactive dish. Combine the red wine, raspberry vinegar, soy sauce, garlic and rosemary in a bowl and mix well. Pour over the lamb, turning to coat. Marinate, covered, in the refrigerator for 8 to 10 hours, turning occasionally. Drain, reserving the marinade.

Preheat the oven to 400 degrees. Roll the lamb leg and secure with kitchen twine. Arrange in a baking pan. Coat the surface of the lamb with the Dijon mustard and pat the peppercorns over the mustard; press lightly. Pour the reserved marinade over the lamb. Reduce the oven temperature to 350 degrees and bake for 18 minutes per pound for rare, basting occasionally. Bake for 10 to 15 minutes longer for well done. Let stand for 20 minutes before carving. Serve with a pinot noir. Yield: 8 servings.

The International Cook Keeps These Flavors on Hand

Cuisine	Flavors
Asian	five-spice powder, ginger, mushrooms, rice wine vinegar, soy
Indian	anise, cardamom, cinnamon, chiles, ginger, mint, tamarind
Italian	basil, fennel seeds, garlic, oregano, Parmesan
Mediterranean	feta cheese, fresh herbs, olives, tomatoes
Mexican	cilantro, chile peppers, lime, salt, tomatoes

Applejack Pork and Sauerkraut

1 (5-pound) center-cut pork loin
Olive oil
3 (32-ounce) cans sauerkraut
2 cups applesauce
2 cups applejack brandy
2 onions, chopped
1/2 cup packed brown sugar
2 cups white wine

Brown the pork on all sides in olive oil in a skillet. Combine the undrained sauerkraut, applesauce, brandy, onions and brown sugar in a bowl and mix well. Spoon into a Dutch oven. Arrange the pork over the sauerkraut mixture. Simmer over low heat for 4 to 5 hours or until the pork is tender, adding the wine throughout the cooking process. Serve with a zinfandel. Yield: 6 to 8 servings.

Pork Tenderloin in Horseradish Crust

1 cup fresh bread crumbs
Salt and pepper to taste
1 tablespoon olive oil
3 tablespoons drained prepared horseradish
1 teaspoon rosemary
1 (2- to 2^1/$_2$-pound) boneless pork tenderloin
1 tablespoon olive oil
1^1/$_2$ teaspoons Dijon mustard

Sauté the bread crumbs, salt and pepper in 1 tablespoon olive oil in a skillet over medium heat until the bread crumbs are golden brown. Combine the bread crumb mixture, horseradish and rosemary in a bowl and mix well.

Pat the pork dry with a paper towel. Sprinkle with salt and pepper. Brown the pork on all sides in 1 tablespoon olive oil in a skillet. Remove the pork to a baking pan. Coat the top and sides of the pork with the Dijon mustard. Pat with the bread crumb mixture and press lightly.

Roast the pork at 425 degrees until a meat thermometer inserted in the center of the pork registers 155 degrees, covering loosely with foil if the bread crumbs begin to overbrown. Let stand for 5 minutes before cutting into ^{1}/$_4$-inch slices. Serve with a chardonnay.
Yield: 4 to 6 servings.

Polynesian Pork Centennial

From The Bethlehem Club, Bethlehem

6 pork chops
Salt and pepper to taste
1 (16-ounce) can juice-pack
    or syrup-pack pineapple
    chunks
12 prunes, pitted
1 onion, chopped
1/4 cup minced celery leaves
1 garlic clove, minced
2 teaspoons soy sauce
1/2 teaspoon marjoram
1 cup diagonally chopped
    celery
1 cup white rice
1 teaspoon freshly grated
    gingerroot

Trim the excess fat from the pork chops. Grease a heavy skillet with fat from 1 pork chop, discarding the remaining fat. Brown the pork chops on both sides in the greased skillet; drain. Sprinkle lightly with salt and pepper.

Drain the pineapple, reserving the juice. Combine the juice, prunes, onion, celery leaves, garlic, soy sauce and marjoram in a bowl and mix well. Pour over the pork chops. Simmer, covered, for 20 to 30 minutes or until the pork chops are almost cooked through, stirring occasionally. Stir in the pineapple and celery.

Cook for 10 minutes longer or until the celery is tender and the pork chops are cooked through, adding a small amount of water if the mixture becomes too dry. Prepare the rice using package directions and adding the gingerroot. Serve the pork chops over the rice with a beaujolais nouveau.
Yield: 6 servings.

Barbecued Spareribs

3 to 4 pounds spareribs
1 tablespoon salt
1/2 teaspoon red pepper
1/2 teaspoon black pepper
2 small onions, sliced
3/4 cup ketchup
3/4 cup water
2 tablespoons vinegar
2 tablespoons Worcestershire sauce
1 teaspoon paprika
1 teaspoon chili powder

Cut the spareribs into serving portions. Sprinkle with the salt, red pepper and black pepper. Arrange in a baking pan. Bake at 450 degrees just until brown; drain. Reduce the oven temperature to 350 degrees. Arrange the onions over the spareribs.

Combine the ketchup, water, vinegar, Worcestershire sauce, paprika and chili powder in a bowl and mix well. Pour over the spareribs. Bake, tightly covered, for 1 1/4 hours, basting occasionally; remove cover. Bake for 15 minutes longer. Serve with a hearty zinfandel.
Yield: 8 servings.

Mom Topp's Sausage and Peppers

2 pounds andouille, hot Italian or other sausage
2 pounds onions, cut into quarters
1/2 head garlic, sliced
Olive oil
16 ounces fresh mushrooms, sliced
2 to 21/2 pounds red and green bell peppers,
    cut into 2-inch pieces
1 to 2 hot peppers, minced
1/4 to 1/2 cup wine vinegar
1 to 2 teaspoons balsamic vinegar
1 tablespoon oregano
Salt and pepper to taste

Brown the sausage in a skillet; drain. Cut into 11/2-inch slices. Sauté the onions and garlic in olive oil in a Dutch oven until the onions are tender. Stir in the mushrooms. Cook for 5 minutes, stirring occasionally.

Add the bell peppers, hot peppers, wine vinegar, balsamic vinegar, oregano, salt and pepper and mix well. Stir in the sausage. Simmer for 30 minutes, stirring occasionally. May cook in a slow cooker on Low for 4 to 5 hours. Serve with a chianti. Yield: 6 to 8 servings.

Crispy Coconut Chicken with Roasted Red Pepper Sauce

1 red bell pepper, roasted
and chopped
1 tablespoon olive oil
1/2 teaspoon fresh lemon
juice
1/4 teaspoon sugar
Cayenne pepper to taste
Salt and black pepper
to taste
1 garlic clove, minced
1/4 teaspoon salt
1 tablespoon Dijon mustard
1/8 teaspoon ground ginger
2 (5-ounce) boneless
skinless chicken breasts
Flour
1 egg
1 teaspoon water
1 cup flaked coconut
2 tablespoons unsalted
butter
2 tablespoons dry
sherry

Process the bell pepper, olive oil, lemon juice, sugar, cayenne pepper, salt and black pepper to taste in a blender until puréed. Mash the garlic with 1/4 teaspoon salt in a small bowl until a paste forms. Stir in the Dijon mustard and ginger. Spread the garlic mixture over both sides of the chicken breasts.

Combine flour, salt and black pepper in a shallow dish and mix well. Whisk the egg with the water in a bowl until blended. Coat the chicken with the flour mixture and shake off the excess. Dip in the egg wash. Pat the coconut over the chicken and press lightly.

Heat the butter in an ovenproof skillet over medium-high heat until the foam subsides. Add the chicken. Sauté for 2 minutes on each side or until the coconut is golden brown. Stir in the sherry. Bake at 375 degrees for 10 to 12 minutes or until the chicken is cooked through. Divide the red pepper sauce evenly between 2 serving plates. Arrange the chicken over the sauce. Serve with a fumé blanc. Yield: 2 servings.

Chicken Elizabeth

6 tablespoons (3/4 stick) butter
6 to 8 boneless skinless chicken breasts
2 cups sour cream
8 ounces bleu cheese, crumbled
1 tablespoon Worcestershire sauce
3 small garlic cloves, crushed

Heat the butter in a large heavy skillet over medium-high heat until melted. Add the chicken. Cook for 4 minutes per side or until brown, turning once. Remove the chicken to a greased 9×13-inch baking dish.

Combine the sour cream, bleu cheese, Worcestershire sauce and garlic in a bowl and mix well. Spread the sour cream mixture over the chicken. Bake at 350 degrees for 50 minutes or until the juices run clear when the chicken is pricked with a fork. Serve over rice with a beaujolais. Yield: 6 to 8 servings.

Roasting Bell Peppers

To roast bell peppers, pierce the bell peppers with a long-handled fork. Char over an open flame for 2 to 3 minutes or until the skin is blistered and blackened on all sides, turning constantly. Or broil the peppers 2 inches from the heat source for 15 to 25 minutes or until the skin is blistered and charred, turning every 5 minutes. Remove the bell peppers to a bowl or a nonrecycled brown paper bag. Let stand, covered or sealed tightly, until cool enough to handle. Peel starting at the blossom end, cut off the tops and discard the seeds and membranes, keeping the peppers whole or chopping, depending on the recipe. Wear rubber gloves when handling chiles.

Potato-Crusted Chicken with Creamy Dijon Sauce

From O'Hara's Pub, Allentown

Chicken
2 large potatoes, peeled
  and shredded
Salt to taste
6 to 8 ounces boneless
  skinless chicken breasts,
  trimmed
Flour
1 egg
1 teaspoon water
Vegetable oil

For the chicken, combine the shredded potatoes with enough salt water to cover in a bowl. Pound the chicken 1/2 inch thick between sheets of waxed paper. Pat dry with a paper towel. Coat with flour and dip in a mixture of the egg and water.

Drain the potatoes. Pack both sides of the chicken with the shredded potatoes. Brown the chicken in a small amount of oil in a skillet. Test to see if the chicken is cooked through. Bake at 350 degrees for 8 minutes or until cooked through if needed. Remove to a serving platter. Cover to keep warm.

Creamy Dijon Sauce
1 teaspoon butter
1/2 teaspoon chopped garlic
1/2 cup white wine
2 cups heavy cream
2 tablespoons Dijon
  mustard
Salt and pepper to taste

For the sauce, combine the butter and garlic in a sauté pan. Sauté just until the garlic is tender; do not brown. Stir in the white wine. Cook until the mixture is reduced by half, stirring constantly. Stir in the cream and Dijon mustard. Cook until thickened and reduced by half, stirring constantly. Season with salt and pepper. Drizzle over the chicken. Serve with a fumé blanc. Yield: 6 to 8 servings.

White-Lights-on-the-Parkway Chili

1 medium onion, chopped
1 garlic clove, minced
1 teaspoon cumin
1/4 teaspoon cinnamon
1 tablespoon vegetable oil
2 whole large boneless skinless chicken breasts,
    cut into bite-size pieces
1 1/2 cups water
1 (16-ounce) can garbanzo beans, drained
1 (16-ounce) can white kidney beans, drained
1 (16-ounce) can white corn kernels, drained
2 (4-ounce) cans chopped green chiles, drained
2 chicken bouillon cubes
Shredded Monterey Jack cheese
Chopped tomatoes

Sauté the onion, garlic, cumin and cinnamon in the oil in a
skillet. Stir in the chicken, water, beans, corn, chiles and
bouillon cubes. Spoon into a baking dish. Bake at 350
degrees for 50 to 60 minutes or until the chicken is cooked
through and the chili is of the desired consistency. Spoon
into chili bowls. Top each serving with shredded cheese
and chopped tomatoes. Serve with a gewürztraminer.
Yield: 10 to 12 servings.

Coconut Ginger Halibut with Thai Sauce

2 cups cold water
1 cup jasmine rice
4 (4-ounce) halibut fillets
    or steaks
Vegetable oil
Salt and pepper to taste
1 (14-ounce) can
    coconut milk
1 tablespoon lime juice
2 (quarter-size) pieces
    gingerroot, peeled,
    finely minced
1 1/2 tablespoons Thai red
    curry base
1 cup chicken broth
1 1/2 teaspoons soy sauce
4 green onions, sliced
Sprigs of cilantro

Combine the cold water and jasmine rice in a
2-quart saucepan; cover. Bring to a boil; reduce the
heat. Simmer for 15 minutes or until the rice is
tender and the water is absorbed.

Brush both sides of the fillets with oil. Season with
salt and pepper. Grill over medium-hot coals for
5 minutes; turn. Grill until the fillets flake easily;
grilling time should equal 10 minutes per inch
of thickness.

Combine the coconut milk, lime juice, gingerroot
and curry base in a saucepan and mix well. Bring
to a boil; reduce heat. Simmer for 5 minutes, stirring
frequently. Stir in the broth and soy sauce. Simmer
for 10 minutes longer, stirring occasionally.

To assemble, divide the rice evenly among
4 shallow bowls. Place 1 fillet in each bowl. Ladle
the sauce over the fish and rice. Sprinkle with the
green onions and top with sprigs of cilantro. Serve
with a mild riesling. Yield: 4 servings.

Ultimate Grilled Fish

1 cup mayonnaise
1 small onion, thinly sliced
2 tablespoons coarse ground mustard
2 tablespoons lemon juice
1 tablespoon wine vinegar
1 teaspoon garlic powder
1 teaspoon of 2 or more herbs (dillweed,
  tarragon, parsley, cilantro or thyme)
4 to 6 tuna, swordfish or salmon steaks
  or fillets

Combine the mayonnaise, onion, ground mustard, lemon juice, wine vinegar, garlic powder and herbs in a bowl and mix well. Spread over both sides of the fish. Arrange in a single layer in a dish. Marinate, covered, in the refrigerator for 30 minutes to several hours.

Place the fish steaks with the thick marinade in place carefully on a grill rack. Grill over hot coals for 3 to 4 minutes per side or until the fish flakes easily. You may broil the fish if desired. Serve with a chardonnay.
Yield: 4 to 6 servings.

Pineapple and Onion Salsa

Combine 1 chopped fresh pineapple, 1 chopped medium onion, 6 tablespoons finely chopped fresh mint, and salt and pepper to taste in a bowl and mix well. Chill, covered, for 8 hours. Adjust the seasonings. Serve with grilled fish or chicken or with tortilla chips. Yield: 3 cups.

Sand Island Clams and Angel Hair Pasta

1 medium onion, chopped
2 tablespoons (heaping) chopped fresh parsley
4 garlic cloves, minced
1/4 cup olive oil
1 (15-ounce) can chicken broth
1 tablespoon flour
1/2 cup dry white wine
3 (7-ounce) cans chopped clams
1 teaspoon salt
1 teaspoon black pepper
16 ounces angel hair pasta
5 tablespoons olive oil
1/2 cup freshly grated Parmesan cheese
Crushed red pepper (optional)

Sauté the onion, parsley and garlic in 1/4 cup olive oil in a skillet over medium-high heat for 10 minutes or until the onion is almost tender. Stir in a mixture of the broth and flour. Cook for 10 minutes, stirring frequently. Add the white wine. Cook for 10 minutes, stirring frequently. Stir in the clams, salt and black pepper. Cook over medium heat for 5 minutes; keep warm until ready to serve.

Cook the pasta using package directions; drain. Toss the pasta with 5 tablespoons olive oil and the cheese in a pasta bowl. Top with the clam sauce. Sprinkle with crushed red pepper. Serve the pasta with a pinot grigio.
Yield: 8 servings.

Zesty Oyster Stew

3/4 cup (1¹/2 sticks) butter
1 teaspoon salt
1 teaspoon black pepper
1/2 teaspoon cayenne pepper
1/8 teaspoon garlic powder
2 tablespoons chopped fresh parsley
2 tablespoons chopped fresh chives or scallions
1¹/2 quarts oyster liquor
4 cups half-and-half
1 cup heavy cream
4 dozen stewing oysters

Heat the butter in a stockpot over medium-low heat. Stir in the salt, black pepper, cayenne pepper, garlic powder, parsley and chives. Sauté for 3 minutes. Stir in the oyster liquor. Cook for 5 minutes over medium heat, stirring frequently.

Add the half-and-half and cream and mix well. Cook for 5 minutes, stirring constantly. Stir in the oysters and cover. Remove from heat. Let stand for 5 minutes. Serve over buttered toast points with Champagne or sparkling wine. Yield: 10 to 12 servings.

Food and Wine Pairings

The old rule for pairing wine and food is "White with light foods" and "Red with rich foods." We don't subscribe to that philosophy. Serve and drink what you and your guests will most enjoy!

145

Shrimp Penne with Crostini

From The Apollo Grill, Bethlehem

*2 cups (4 sticks) unsalted
    butter, softened*
*1/4 cup chopped
    fresh parsley*
*1 tablespoon chopped
    fresh basil*
*5 garlic cloves, finely
    chopped*
1 shallot, finely chopped
Salt and pepper to taste
1/4 cup olive oil
1 large red onion, julienned
*2 pounds shrimp, peeled
    and deveined*
*2 bunches asparagus,
    diagonally cut into
    1-inch slices, blanched*
*16 ounces penne, cooked
    al dente*
*Freshly grated Parmesan
    cheese*
1 loaf French bread

Combine the butter, parsley, basil, garlic, shallot, salt and pepper in a bowl and mix well. Chill the garlic butter, covered, in the refrigerator.

Heat the olive oil in a large sauté pan over medium-high heat. Add the onion. Cook until tender, stirring frequently. Add the shrimp, salt and pepper. Cook just until the shrimp turn pink, stirring frequently. Add the asparagus and 1/4 of the garlic butter. Combine with the pasta in a bowl and toss to mix. Add salt, pepper, cheese and additional garlic butter if desired.

Cut the bread diagonally into 1-inch slices. Arrange in a single layer on a baking sheet. Heat the remaining garlic butter in a saucepan until melted. Brush both sides of the bread slices with some of the garlic butter. Bake at 375 degrees until crispy. Remove from oven. Top with any of the following: fresh mozzarella cheese, basil and roasted peppers; arugula, walnuts and goat cheese; fresh tomatoes or scallions and Parmesan cheese. Bake until the cheese melts. Serve the crostini with the pasta along with a chardonnay of your choice. Yield: 6 to 8 servings.

Shrimp Scampi with Red Bell Pepper and Zucchini

3/4 cup (1 1/2 sticks) butter
2 red bell peppers, cut into 1/2×2-inch strips
12 ounces zucchini, cut into 1/2-inch slices
3/4 cup chopped shallots
1/4 cup finely chopped garlic
1/4 cup drained capers
2 pounds large shrimp with tails, peeled and deveined
1/3 cup chopped fresh basil

Heat the butter in a large heavy skillet over high heat.
Add the bell peppers, zucchini, shallots and garlic. Sauté
for 4 minutes or just until the shallots begin to soften. Stir
in the capers. Spoon into a baking dish or gratin dish.
May be prepared in advance up to this point and cooled.
Cover and set aside until just before baking.

Stir the shrimp into the vegetable mixture. Bake at
450 degrees for 10 minutes or until the shrimp turn pink,
stirring occasionally. Sprinkle with the basil. Serve with a
sauvignon blanc. Yield: 8 servings.

Bouillabaisse

3 tablespoons olive oil
2 large tomatoes, chopped
4 large shallots, chopped
1 leek, chopped
4 garlic cloves, minced
1 gallon shrimp stock
1 cup sherry
4 (3-ounce) lobster tails
20 littleneck clams
20 mussels
8 large shrimp
4 (6-ounce) sole fillets
12 oysters
12 large sea scallops
1 bunch scallions, chopped
8 ounces lump crab meat
Saffron to taste
Salt and pepper to taste
Tabasco sauce to taste

Heat the olive oil in a large stockpot over high heat. Add the tomatoes, shallots, leek and garlic. Sauté for 2 minutes; reduce heat to low. Stir in the stock and sherry. Simmer for 3 minutes, stirring occasionally.

Add the lobster. Simmer, covered, for 5 minutes, stirring occasionally. Add the clams. Simmer, covered, for 2 minutes. Stir in the mussels, shrimp and sole.

Simmer, covered, until the shrimp turn pink and the mussels open. Stir in the oysters, scallops and scallions. Simmer for 3 minutes, stirring occasionally.

Add the crab meat. Simmer just until heated through. Stir in the saffron, salt, pepper and Tabasco sauce. Ladle into soup bowls. Serve with a merlot. Yield: 8 servings.

Christmas City Seafood Stew

¹/₂ cup chopped onion
¹/₂ cup chopped red bell pepper
1 garlic clove, minced
1 (14-ounce) can diced tomatoes
1 (15-ounce) can tomato sauce
¹/₄ cup burgundy or dry red wine
¹/₄ cup chopped fresh oregano
2 tablespoons chopped fresh parsley
1 teaspoon Worcestershire sauce
¹/₄ teaspoon crushed red pepper
8 ounces bay scallops
8 ounces medium shrimp, peeled, deveined
1 (10-ounce) can salty whole clams

Coat a Dutch oven with nonstick cooking spray. Heat over medium-high heat until hot. Add the onion, bell pepper and garlic. Sauté for 5 minutes or until the onion is tender. Stir in the undrained tomatoes, tomato sauce and wine. Add the oregano, parsley, Worcestershire sauce and red pepper. Bring to a boil over medium heat; reduce heat.

Simmer, covered, for 20 minutes, stirring occasionally. Stir in the scallops, shrimp and clams. Bring to a boil; reduce heat. Simmer for 7 to 8 minutes or until the scallops are tender and the shrimp turn pink, stirring occasionally. Ladle into soup bowls. The stew may be prepared in advance and stored, covered, in the refrigerator, adding the seafood just before serving. Double the recipe for large crowds, but it is best not to double the amount of crushed red pepper. Serve with a hearty zinfandel. Yield: 12 servings.

Lehigh River Lasagna

3 (8-ounce) cans tomato sauce
1 (16-ounce) can pinto beans, rinsed and drained
1/2 cup finely chopped green bell pepper
1/4 cup finely chopped onion
15 small pitted black olives, sliced
1 teaspoon vinegar
1/2 teaspoon oregano
1/2 teaspoon cumin
1/4 teaspoon garlic powder
6 (6-inch) corn tortillas, cut into quarters
1 cup shredded Cheddar cheese

Spray a 7×11-inch baking pan with nonstick cooking spray.
Spread 1/4 cup of the tomato sauce in the prepared pan.
Combine the remaining tomato sauce, pinto beans, bell
pepper, onion, olives, vinegar, oregano, cumin and garlic
powder in a bowl and mix well.

Layer the tortillas, tomato sauce mixture and cheese
1/3 at a time in the prepared baking pan. Bake, covered,
at 375 degrees for 20 minutes; remove the cover. Bake for
15 minutes longer. Let stand for 5 minutes before serving.
Serve with sangria or a chianti. Yield: 8 servings.

Greek Penne Pasta

5 garlic cloves, minced
1 tablespoon olive oil
4 cups fresh spinach,
    chopped
2 (4-ounce) cans sliced
    black olives, drained
4 large plum tomatoes,
    chopped
4 ounces feta cheese,
    crumbled
1/2 cup cottage cheese
16 ounces penne, cooked,
    drained
1 tablespoon olive oil
Salt and pepper to taste
2 tablespoons pine nuts

Sauté the garlic in 1 tablespoon olive oil in a skillet; do not brown. Stir in the spinach, olives and tomatoes. Cook for 30 minutes, stirring occasionally. Combine the feta cheese and cottage cheese in a bowl and mix well.

Toss the pasta with 1 tablespoon olive oil in a bowl. Stir in the spinach mixture and feta cheese mixture. Season with salt and pepper. Sprinkle with the pine nuts. Serve immediately with a sauvignon blanc. Yield: 8 servings.

Traditional Pesto

3 cups loosely packed fresh
    basil
3/4 cup olive oil
1/4 cup pine nuts
3 garlic cloves
1/2 cup freshly grated
    Parmesan cheese

Combine the basil, olive oil, pine nuts and garlic in a food processor or blender container. Process until smooth. Pour into a bowl. Stir in the cheese. Spoon over 8 ounces of your favorite hot cooked pasta on a serving platter. Serve hot or cold. Yield: 3 cups.

Tortellini in Basil Cream Sauce

2 (4-ounce) packages fresh tortellini
1/2 cup (1 stick) butter
2 garlic cloves, minced
1/4 cup chopped fresh basil
2 tablespoons chopped fresh parsley
1 cup light cream
2/3 cup mayonnaise
2 egg yolks, beaten
Salt and pepper to taste
2/3 cup chopped prosciutto
1/2 cup grated Parmesan cheese

Cook the pasta using package directions for 5 to 8 minutes; drain. Cover to keep warm. Heat the butter in a saucepan until melted. Stir in the garlic, basil and parsley. Cook over low heat until the garlic is tender, stirring constantly.

Combine the cream, mayonnaise, egg yolks, salt and pepper in a bowl and mix well. Stir into the butter mixture. Add the prosciutto and mix well.

Cook for 5 to 10 minutes over low heat or until of the desired consistency, stirring frequently. Toss the tortellini and cheese in a bowl. Add the sauce and mix well. Serve immediately with a sauvignon blanc. Yield: 6 to 8 servings.

Fall Foliage Vegetable Stew

1 tablespoon vegetable oil
4 cups mushrooms, cut into quarters
1¹/2 cups sliced onions
1 cup each (1-inch) slices carrot and celery
2 garlic cloves, minced
1 (16-ounce) can whole tomatoes
3 unpeeled medium potatoes, cut into 1-inch chunks
2 cups cooked kidney beans
1 (8-ounce) can tomato sauce
1 cup water
1 teaspoon thyme
1 bay leaf
Salt and pepper to taste
2 tablespoons flour
¹/4 cup each water and red wine

Heat the oil in a large heavy saucepan over medium heat. Add the mushrooms, onions, carrot, celery and garlic. Cook for 10 minutes, stirring frequently. Add small amounts of water if needed to prevent the vegetables from sticking. Chop the tomatoes coarsely, reserving the juice. Stir the potatoes, tomatoes and juice, beans, tomato sauce, 1 cup water, thyme, bay leaf, salt and pepper into the saucepan.

Simmer, covered, over low heat for 30 minutes or until the vegetables are tender, stirring occasionally. Stir the flour into ¹/4 cup water in a bowl until blended. Stir into the stew. Add the red wine and mix well. Cook for 5 minutes longer, stirring constantly. Discard the bay leaf. Ladle into soup bowls or hollowed pumpkins (see page 27). Serve with an Australian shiraz. Yield: 10 servings.

THE CHILDREN'S
ADVOCACY CENTER

Perhaps our greatest contribution to the Lehigh Valley is still to come. Since 1995, the JLLV has been working closely with other community and government agencies toward the establishment of an advocacy center solely for the benefit and care of children.

The goal remains to have a multidisciplinary team in place, in one site, to provide child victims of sexual abuse with a nonthreatening, comforting environment where they may receive an array of necessary services, including medical exams, investigative interviews, crisis therapy, and support.

Elegant
ENDINGS

Apricot Pound Cake

Cake
3 cups flour
1/2 teaspoon salt
1/4 teaspoon baking soda
1 cup (2 sticks) butter,
    softened
3 cups sugar
6 eggs
1 cup sour cream
2/3 cup apricot brandy
1 1/2 teaspoons rum
1 teaspoon vanilla extract
1 teaspoon orange extract

For the cake, combine the flour, salt and baking soda in a bowl; set aside. Cream the butter and sugar in a large mixing bowl until light and fluffy. Add the eggs 1 at a time, beating well after each addition. Add the sour cream, brandy, rum, vanilla and orange extract; mix well. Add the flour mixture and beat until well blended. Pour into a greased tube pan.

Bake at 350 degrees for 1 1/4 hours or until a wooden pick inserted in the cake comes out clean. Let cool. Invert the cake onto a serving plate. Serve the Apricot Topping over the cake. Yield: 16 servings.

Apricot Topping
1 cup dried apricots,
    chopped
1/2 cup orange juice
1/4 cup (1/2 stick) butter
1/2 cup packed brown sugar
2 teaspoons milk
1 tablespoon cornstarch

For the topping, soak the apricots in the orange juice in a bowl; set aside. Melt the butter in a saucepan over medium heat. Add the brown sugar, milk and cornstarch. Cook until thickened, stirring occasionally. Add the apricot and orange juice mixture. Cook until the apricots are softened. Let cool completely.

Flourless Chocolate Cake with Raspberry Coulis

8 eggs, cold
16 (1-ounce) squares bittersweet chocolate
1 cup (2 sticks) unsalted butter, cut into
*   1/2-inch pieces*
Raspberry Coulis (at right)

Adjust the oven rack to the lower-middle position. Line the bottom of an 8-inch springform pan with waxed paper. Grease the side of the pan. Cover the outside bottom and side of the pan with foil. Set aside. Beat the eggs in a large mixing bowl for 5 minutes. Combine the chocolate and butter in a microwave-safe bowl. Microwave on Medium for 4 to 6 minutes or until melted, stirring once or twice. Fold the beaten eggs into the chocolate mixture 1/3 at a time until well blended. Pour into the prepared pan. Set in a larger pan. Pour enough boiling water into the larger pan to come halfway up the side of the springform pan.

Bake at 325 degrees for 20 to 25 minutes or until a thermometer inserted in the center reaches 140 degrees and the edges have set. Cool on a wire rack. Remove the foil. Chill, covered, for up to 4 days. Remove the bottom and side of the pan and invert the cake onto waxed paper. Peel the waxed paper from the bottom of the cake. Invert the cake onto a serving plate. Serve with the Raspberry Coulis. Yield: 12 servings.

Raspberry Coulis

Crush 1/2 cup fresh or frozen raspberries in a saucepan. Add 2/3 cup water and bring to a boil. Reduce the heat and simmer for 2 minutes. Strain the mixture to remove the seeds. Return to the saucepan. Stir in 1/3 cup sugar and 1 tablespoon cornstarch. Cook until thickened, stirring constantly. Cook for 2 minutes, stirring constantly. Remove from heat. Stir in 1 1/2 cups fresh or frozen raspberries and 1/4 teaspoon vanilla extract.

Mrs. Savell's Carrot Cake with Cream Cheese Frosting

Cake

2 cups flour
2 teaspoons baking soda
2 teaspoons cinnamon
1 teaspoon salt
2 cups sugar
1½ cups vegetable oil
4 eggs
3 cups grated carrots

For the cake, sift the flour, baking soda, cinnamon and salt together. Beat the sugar and oil in a large mixing bowl. Add the flour mixture and beat well. Add the eggs 1 at a time, beating well after each addition. Stir in the carrots. Pour into 2 greased and floured 9-inch round cake pans.

Bake at 350 degrees for 30 to 45 minutes or until a wooden pick inserted in the center comes out clean. Invert onto a wire rack to cool completely. Spread the Cream Cheese Frosting between the layers and over the top and side of the cooled cake. Yield: 12 servings.

Cream Cheese Frosting

8 ounces cream cheese, softened
½ cup (1 stick) margarine, softened
1 (1-pound) package confectioners' sugar
1 teaspoon vanilla extract
1 cup chopped pecans (optional)

For the frosting, beat the cream cheese and margarine in a mixing bowl. Add the confectioners' sugar and beat until light and fluffy. Beat in the vanilla. Add the pecans. You may also sprinkle pecans over the top of the frosted cake if desired.

Buckeyes

1 cup creamy peanut butter
1 cup (2 sticks) butter,
    softened
1 (1-pound) package
    confectioners' sugar
2 cups semisweet chocolate
    chips

Beat the peanut butter and butter in a large mixing bowl. Add the confectioners' sugar and beat until well blended. Chill in the refrigerator. Shape into balls and place in a single layer on a baking sheet. You may freeze at this point for up to 2 months.

Melt the chocolate chips in a double boiler. Insert a wooden pick into each ball. Dip the balls in the chocolate, do not coat the top. Place on waxed paper. Remove the wooden picks and smooth the holes. Yield: 24 servings.

Chocolate Toffee Bark

6 to 8 graham crackers
1 cup (2 sticks) butter
1 cup packed brown sugar
1 cup chopped pecans
2 cups semisweet chocolate
    chips

Line a 10×15-inch baking pan with foil. Line the pan with the graham crackers. Melt the butter in a saucepan. Add the brown sugar and pecans and mix well. Bring to a boil. Cook for 3 minutes. Pour over the graham crackers.

Bake at 375 degrees for 8 minutes; do not burn the sugar. Top with the chocolate chips. Bake for 1 or 2 minutes or until the chocolate chips are melted. Spread the chocolate chips evenly over the top. Let cool. Break into pieces. Store in an airtight container in the refrigerator or freezer. Yield: 10 servings.

Rum Balls

1 (12-ounce) package
   vanilla wafers, crushed
1 cup chopped pecans or
   walnuts
2 tablespoons baking cocoa
$^1/_4$ cup rum
1 cup confectioners' sugar

Combine the wafers and pecans in a large bowl. Add the baking cocoa and rum and mix well. Shape into 1-inch balls and roll in the confectioners' sugar. Store in an airtight container in the refrigerator. Yield: 36 servings.

Virginia Fudge

$2^1/_2$ cups sugar
$^3/_4$ cup evaporated milk
$^1/_4$ cup ($^1/_2$ stick) butter
16 marshmallows
2 cups milk chocolate chips
1 teaspoon vanilla extract
1 cup chopped walnuts

Combine the sugar, evaporated milk, butter and marshmallows in a saucepan. Bring to a boil. Boil for 5 minutes. Add the chocolate chips and vanilla, stirring until the chocolate chips are melted. Stir in the walnuts.

Pour into a buttered 9×12-inch pan. Cool completely in the refrigerator. Cut into 1-inch squares to serve. Yield: 24 servings.

Almond Biscotti

1 cup sugar
¹/₄ cup (¹/₂ stick) margarine, softened
3 eggs
1 tablespoon almond extract
2 cups plus 3 tablespoons flour
2 teaspoons baking powder
¹/₂ teaspoon salt
1 (8-ounce) package slivered almonds

Cream the sugar and margarine in a large mixing bowl until light and fluffy. Add the eggs 1 at a time, beating well after each addition. Beat in the almond extract. Mix the flour, baking powder and salt together. Add the flour mixture to the egg mixture gradually, beating at low speed, mixing well after each addition. Stir in the almonds.

Divide the batter into 2 equal portions. Shape each portion into a long narrow rectangle. Place on greased baking sheets. Bake at 375 degrees for 15 to 20 minutes or until golden brown. Remove from the baking sheets and cut into 1-inch slices. Return the slices cut side down to the baking sheets. Bake for 10 to 15 minutes. Remove to a wire rack to cool. Yield: 16 servings.

Timing

When selecting recipes for your entertaining, review preparation and cooking times. Choose recipes that can be made wholly or partially in advance so you can enjoy being with your guests. For any last-minute preparations, get your chopping done ahead of time. Your guests will be more comfortable if you are not held hostage in the kitchen.

Oatmeal Cranberry Cookies

1 cup (2 sticks) unsalted butter, softened
1¼ cups packed brown sugar
½ cup sugar
2 eggs
2 tablespoons milk
2 teaspoons vanilla extract
2½ cups rolled oats
2 cups flour
1 teaspoon baking soda
1 teaspoon cinnamon
1 teaspoon salt
2 cups dried cranberries

Cream the butter, brown sugar and sugar in a large mixing bowl until light and fluffy. Beat in the eggs, milk and vanilla. Combine the oats, flour, baking soda, cinnamon and salt in a large bowl. Add the oat mixture to the creamed mixture gradually, mixing well after each addition. Stir in the cranberries.

Drop by rounded tablespoonfuls onto a cookie sheet. Bake at 350 degrees for 10 to 12 minutes or until golden brown. Yield: 24 servings.

Oatmeal Caramelitas

1 cup flour
1 cup rolled oats
³/4 cup packed brown sugar
¹/2 teaspoon baking soda
¹/4 teaspoon salt
³/4 cup (1¹/2 sticks) butter, melted
1 cup semisweet chocolate chips
³/4 cup chopped pecans
³/4 cup caramel topping
3 tablespoons flour

Combine the flour, oats, brown sugar, baking soda and salt in a large bowl. Add the melted butter and mix well. Divide into 2 equal portions. Press half the oat mixture into a greased 9-inch baking pan. Bake at 350 degrees for 10 minutes.

Sprinkle the chocolate chips and pecans over the crust. Combine the caramel topping and flour in a small bowl and mix well. Pour over the top. Top with the remaining oat mixture.

Bake at 350 degrees for 15 to 20 minutes or until set. Chill in the refrigerator before cutting into squares. Yield: 24 servings.

Scottish Shortbread

1¹/₂ cups (3 sticks) unsalted butter, softened
1 cup confectioners' sugar
3 cups sifted flour
¹/₂ teaspoon salt
1 teaspoon vanilla extract
¹/₄ cup sugar

Cream the butter and confectioners' sugar in a large
mixing bowl until light and fluffy. Combine the flour and salt
in a bowl. Add to the creamed mixture gradually, mixing
well after each addition. Add the vanilla and beat well.
Shape the dough into a ball and wrap in plastic wrap. Chill
for 4 to 6 hours.

Roll the dough ³/₈ inch thick. Cut into desired shapes with
cookie cutters. Place on cookie sheets and sprinkle the
tops with the sugar. Chill for 30 minutes.

Bake at 325 degrees for 20 minutes or until light golden
brown. Remove to a wire rack to cool. Yield: 24 servings.

White Chocolate Orange Dream Cookies

1 cup (2 sticks) butter, softened
1/2 cup packed brown sugar
1/2 cup sugar
1 egg
Grated zest of 1 orange
2 1/4 cups flour
3/4 teaspoon baking soda
1/2 teaspoon salt
2 cups white chocolate chips

Cream the butter, brown sugar and sugar in a large
mixing bowl until light and fluffy. Add the egg and orange
zest and beat well. Combine the flour, baking soda and
salt in a bowl. Add the flour mixture to the creamed
mixture gradually, beating until blended after each addition.
Stir in the white chocolate chips. The batter will be stiff.

Drop by spoonfuls onto a cookie sheet. Bake at
350 degrees for 10 to 12 minutes. Let cool on the cookie
sheet for 2 minutes. Remove to a wire rack to cool
completely. Yield: 18 servings.

Chambord Brownies

Brownies
1/2 cup (1 stick) butter,
    softened
1 cup sugar
4 eggs, beaten
1 cup flour
1/2 teaspoon salt
1 (16-ounce) can
    chocolate syrup

For the brownies, cream the butter and sugar in a mixing bowl until light and fluffy. Beat in the eggs. Add the flour and salt gradually, beating until well blended. Beat in the chocolate syrup. Pour into a greased 9×13-inch baking pan. Bake at 350 degrees for 30 minutes. Let cool completely. Spread the Chambord Filling over the cooled brownies. Chill until set. Pour the Chocolate Glaze evenly over the filling. Chill until set. Bring to room temperature before cutting into squares. Yield: 24 servings.

Chambord Filling
2 cups confectioners'
    sugar
1/2 cup (1 stick) butter,
    softened
2 tablespoons Chambord or
    other raspberry-flavor
    liqueur
1/8 teaspoon red
    food coloring

For the filling, cream the confectioners' sugar and butter in a mixing bowl until light and fluffy. Add the liqueur and red food coloring and beat until well blended.

Chocolate Glaze
2 cups semisweet
    chocolate chips
3/4 cup (1 1/2 sticks) butter

For the glaze, melt the chocolate chips and butter in a saucepan over low heat, stirring until smooth.

Nana's Walnut Brownies

1 cup shortening
2 (1-ounce) squares unsweetened baking chocolate
2 cups sugar
2 teaspoons vanilla extract
4 eggs, beaten
1¹/₂ cups cake flour
¹/₄ teaspoon baking powder
¹/₈ teaspoon salt
1 cup chopped walnuts

Melt the shortening and chocolate in a double boiler; set aside. Beat the sugar and vanilla into the eggs in a mixing bowl gradually, mixing well after each addition. Add the chocolate mixture and beat until smooth. Add the flour, baking powder and salt gradually, beating well after each addition. Stir in the walnuts. Pour into 3 greased 8×11-inch baking pans.

Bake at 325 degrees for 20 to 25 minutes or until a wooden pick inserted in the center comes out clean. Let cool and cut into squares. Yield: 24 to 36 servings.

Johnny Appleseed Tart

1 (1-crust) pie pastry, at room temperature
5 Golden Delicious apples, peeled, cored
1/4 cup sugar
1/4 cup (1/2 stick) unsalted butter
1/8 teaspoon cinnamon
3 tablespoons apricot jam
1 tablespoon water

Press the pie pastry into a 9-inch tart pan. Chill, covered, in the refrigerator. Cut the apples into thick slices. Arrange the apples in the pie shell in a decorative pattern. Sprinkle with the sugar and dot with the butter. Sprinkle with the cinnamon. Bake at 375 degrees for 45 minutes or until light golden brown.

Combine the apricot jam and water in a small saucepan. Cook until the jam is melted. Brush the apricot mixture evenly over the warm tart with a pastry brush. Serve warm or at room temperature. Yield: 8 servings.

Praline Apple Pie

6 to 8 cooking apples, peeled, cored, sliced
³/4 cup sugar
¹/3 cup flour
¹/2 teaspoon cinnamon
¹/4 teaspoon salt
1 unbaked (9-inch) pie shell
2 tablespoons butter
1 tablespoon lemon juice
¹/4 cup (¹/2 stick) butter
¹/2 cup packed brown sugar
2 tablespoons heavy cream
¹/2 cup pecans

Combine the apples with the sugar, flour, cinnamon and salt in a bowl and mix well to coat. Spoon into the pie shell. Dot with 2 tablespoons butter and sprinkle with the lemon juice. Bake at 400 degrees for 45 minutes. Remove from the oven.

Melt ¹/4 cup butter in a saucepan. Stir in the brown sugar and cream. Cook over low heat almost to the boiling point, stirring constantly; do not boil. Stir in the pecans. Pour over the top of the pie. Bake for 5 minutes longer. Yield: 8 servings.

Houseguests

Take care of your houseguests. Place fresh flowers in the guest room and the guest bathroom. Leave snacks or special treats by the side of the bed. Make sure there is a clock radio or CD player in the room. Let your guests sleep late. Put sample-size toiletries and pain relievers in the bathroom as well.

Chocolate Chip Bourbon Pecan Pies

1/2 cup (1 stick) butter,
    melted
1 cup light corn syrup
1 cup sugar
4 eggs, beaten
1 to 2 tablespoons bourbon
1/2 cup chocolate chips
1 cup chopped pecans
2 unbaked (9-inch)
    pie shells

Combine the melted butter, corn syrup, sugar, eggs and bourbon in a large bowl and mix well. Stir in the chocolate chips and pecans. Pour into the pie shells. Bake at 350 degrees for 40 to 45 minutes or until set. Serve warm with whipped cream or vanilla ice cream. Yield: 12 to 16 servings.

Nostalgic Strawberry Pie

2 quarts fresh strawberries,
    hulled
1 cup water
1/2 cup sugar
1 tablespoon cornstarch
1 (3-ounce) package
    strawberry gelatin
1 baked (9-inch) pie shell

Rinse the strawberries and cut into halves; set aside. Combine the water, sugar and cornstarch in a saucepan. Cook until thickened, stirring frequently. Remove from heat and stir in the gelatin. Let stand for 10 minutes.

Combine with the strawberries in a large bowl. Chill in the refrigerator for a few minutes if the mixture seems thin. Spoon into the pie shell. Arrange the strawberries cut side down. Chill, covered, until serving time. Serve with whipped cream.
Yield: 8 servings.

Strawberry Kiwifruit Tart with Mint Custard

Walnut Tart Shell

1/2 cup (1 stick) butter, softened
1/3 cup sugar
1 teaspoon vanilla extract
1 cup flour
1/4 cup ground walnuts

For the shell, cream the butter and sugar in a food processor until light and fluffy. Mix in the vanilla. Add the flour and walnuts gradually, processing until the mixture is crumbly. Press the dough over the bottom and up the sides of a 10-inch tart pan. Chill for 30 to 45 minutes. Prick the bottom of the shell with a fork. Line the shell with foil and place pie weights in the bottom. Bake at 375 degrees for 15 minutes. Remove the foil and pie weights and bake for 2 to 3 minutes or until the shell is golden brown.

Mint Custard

2 cups milk
1/2 cup chopped fresh mint leaves
3 egg yolks
1/4 cup sugar
2 tablespoons flour
1 teaspoon vanilla extract

For the custard, combine the milk and mint in a small saucepan. Cook over medium heat almost to the boiling point, stirring frequently. Remove from heat and let sit for 10 minutes. Strain into a bowl, pressing on the mint leaves. Whisk the egg yolks, sugar, flour and vanilla in a medium saucepan over low heat. Add the milk gradually, stirring constantly. Cook almost to the boiling point, stirring constantly. Let cool, stirring occasionally. Chill, covered, for at least 3 hours.

Assembly

1 quart fresh strawberries, rinsed, hulled
3 kiwifruit, peeled, sliced

To assemble, remove the tart shell from the pan and place on a serving plate. Spread a layer of custard in the shell. Place the largest strawberry in the center. Arrange a layer of kiwifruit around the strawberry and continue alternating circles of strawberries and kiwifruit to cover the tart. You may serve additional custard alone or with additional fruit. Yield: 8 servings.

Walnut Torte

3 egg whites, stiffly beaten
20 butter crackers, crushed
1 cup sugar
1/8 teaspoon salt
1/2 cup baking powder
3/4 cup chopped walnuts
1/2 teaspoon vanilla extract
1/2 teaspoon almond extract

Combine the beaten egg whites, butter crackers, sugar,
salt and baking powder in a large bowl and mix well. Stir in
the walnuts, vanilla and almond extract. Pour into a 9-inch
pie plate.

Bake at 325 degrees for 30 to 45 minutes or until a knife
inserted in the center comes out clean. Let cool.

Serve with vanilla ice cream, fresh strawberries or
raspberries and hot fudge sauce. Yield: 8 to 10 servings.

Walnut Lemon Meringue Bombe

1/2 cup sugar
2 egg whites, stiffly beaten
1/4 cup finely chopped walnuts
1 1/4 cups whipping cream
5 tablespoons lemon curd

Whisk half the sugar into the egg whites in a bowl.
Whisk in the remaining sugar. Fold in the walnuts. Press
into a pie plate. Bake at 300 degrees for 1 3/4 hours. Let
cool completely.

Whip 1 cup of the cream and lemon curd in a bowl until
stiff peaks form. Break the meringue shell into pieces and
fold into the cream mixture. Line a mold with plastic wrap.
Spoon the mixture into the mold, smoothing the top. Cover
with plastic wrap. Freeze for 8 to 10 hours.

Invert onto a serving plate. Beat the remaining 1/4 cup
whipping cream until soft peaks form. Frost the dessert
with the whipped cream. Cut into slices to serve.
Yield: 6 to 8 servings.

Apple Streusel Cheesecake

Butter Crust
1/2 cup butter, softened
1/3 cup sugar
1 cup flour

For the crust, cream the butter and sugar in a bowl until light and fluffy. Beat in the flour until well blended. Press over the bottom and 1/2 inch up the side of a greased 9-inch springform pan. Bake at 350 degrees for 12 to 15 minutes or until golden brown.

Filling
3 apples
2 tablespoons butter
1/4 cup sugar
2 tablespoons heavy cream
8 ounces cream cheese
1 lemon
1/2 cup packed brown sugar
2 eggs
1 cup sour cream

For the filling, peel, core and cut the apples into 1/3-inch slices. Melt the butter with the brown sugar in a skillet over medium heat. Sauté the apples for 3 to 5 minutes or until tender and light brown. Add the cream. Cook for 5 minutes, stirring occasionally; set aside. Grate and squeeze the lemon. Beat the cream cheese and brown sugar in a large mixing bowl until smooth. Add the eggs 1 at a time, beating well after each addition. Beat in the sour cream, lemon zest and lemon juice.

Streusel Topping
1/4 cup (1/2 stick) butter,
  softened
1/4 cup packed brown sugar
1/2 cup flour
1/4 teaspoon cinnamon

For the topping, cut the butter into the brown sugar in a mixing bowl until well combined. Mix in the flour and cinnamon until crumbly.

To assemble, arrange the apples over the bottom of the crust using a slotted spoon. Cover with the cream cheese filling. Sprinkle the topping over the filling. Bake at 350 degrees for 45 minutes or until the center is set. Let cool completely. Chill, covered, for 4 to 10 hours. Run a sharp knife around the side of the pan and remove the side carefully.
Yield: 12 servings.

Metro Cheesecake

Vanilla Crust

6 tablespoons (³/4 stick)
    butter, softened
3 tablespoons sugar
³/4 teaspoon vanilla
    extract
³/4 cup flour

Filling

³/4 cup sugar
2 tablespoons flour
¹/8 teaspoon salt
24 ounces cream cheese,
    softened
2 eggs
1 tablespoon vanilla
    extract
¹/2 teaspoon lemon zest
1 cup heavy cream

For the crust, cream the butter and sugar in a mixing bowl until light and fluffy. Beat in the vanilla. Stir in the flour until well blended. Press over the bottom and up the side of a 9-inch springform pan. Bake at 350 degrees for 10 minutes or until golden brown. Let cool completely.

For the filling, combine the sugar, flour and salt in a large mixing bowl. Beat in the cream cheese until smooth. Add the eggs 1 at a time, beating well after each addition. Stir in the vanilla, lemon zest and cream. Pour into the crust. Bake at 350 degrees for 55 minutes. Cool on a wire rack for 1 hour. Run a sharp knife around the side of the pan and remove the side carefully. Chill, covered, for 4 to 5 hours before cutting. Garnish as desired. Yield: 12 servings.

Peanut Butter Cup Cheesecake

Chocolate Crust
2 cups chocolate sandwich
   cookie crumbs
1/4 cup (1/2 stick) butter,
   melted

Filling
32 ounces cream cheese,
   softened
1 1/2 cups packed brown
   sugar
1/2 cup peanut butter
1 teaspoon vanilla extract
4 eggs
2 cups chopped peanut
   butter cups
2 cups sour cream
1/4 cup sugar
1 teaspoon vanilla extract

For the crust, combine the cookie crumbs and melted butter in a bowl and mix well. Press over the bottom and up the side of a 9-inch springform pan. Bake at 350 degrees for 8 minutes. Place the pan on a baking sheet. Let cool.

For the filling, beat the cream cheese, brown sugar, peanut butter and vanilla in a large mixing bowl until well blended. Add the eggs 1 at a time, beating well after each addition. Stir in the peanut butter cup pieces. Pour into the crust. Bake at 325 degrees for 55 minutes. Let cool for 10 minutes.

Beat the sour cream, sugar and vanilla in a small mixing bowl. Spread on top of the cheesecake. Bake for 5 minutes.

Let cool and chill, covered, for 8 to 10 hours. Run a sharp knife around the side of the pan and remove the side carefully. Yield: 12 servings.

Pear Apple Crisp with Cinnamon Crème Anglaise

Crisp

4 medium apples, peeled,
　thinly sliced
4 medium pears, peeled,
　thinly sliced
1 tablespoon sugar
1 to 2 teaspoons lemon
　juice
4 pairs amaretti cookies
1/2 cup flour
1/2 cup packed brown sugar
1/2 teaspoon cinnamon
1/8 teaspoon salt
1/4 cup (1/2 stick) unsalted
　butter

Cinnamon Crème Anglaise

2 cups light cream
1 cinnamon stick
4 egg yolks
1/4 cup sugar
1/2 teaspoon cinnamon

For the crisp, combine the apple and pear slices with the sugar and lemon juice in a bowl and toss well. Arrange in a pie plate or divide evenly among 8 individual ramekins. Crush the amaretti cookies coarsely in their paper wrapping with a rolling pin. Combine the amaretti crumbs, flour, brown sugar, cinnamon and salt in a bowl. Cut in the butter until crumbly. Sprinkle over the fruit.

Bake at 375 degrees for 30 minutes or until the apples are tender and the topping is golden brown. Serve with the Cinnamon Crème Anglaise.
Yield: 8 servings.

For the crème anglaise, combine the cream and cinnamon stick in a small saucepan. Cook over low heat for 10 minutes or until hot but not boiling. Remove the cinnamon stick. Beat the egg yolks and sugar in a mixing bowl. Whisk the hot cream into the egg yolk mixture gradually. Cook over medium heat until the crème anglaise is slightly thickened and coats the back of the spoon, stirring constantly with a wooden spoon. Pour into a bowl and stir in the cinnamon. Strain into a separate bowl. Chill, covered, until cold.

Dutch Chocolate Mousse

Mousse

1 cup semisweet chocolate
   chips
1/2 cup Vandermint or
   other mint-flavor
   liqueur, hot
1 cup (2 sticks) unsalted
   butter, cut into pieces
4 egg yolks
4 egg whites
2 tablespoons confectioners'
   sugar

For the mousse, combine the chocolate chips and liqueur in a blender container. Add the butter and egg yolks. Process until smooth.

Beat the egg whites and confectioners' sugar in a mixing bowl until soft peaks form. Fold in the chocolate mixture.

Pour into a 2-quart soufflé dish or individual soufflé dishes. May also pour into wineglasses or other individual dessert dishes. Cover with plastic wrap and chill until firm.

Top with the whipped cream and garnish with bittersweet chocolate curls immediately before serving. You may substitute egg substitute equivalent to 4 eggs for the eggs.
Yield: 8 servings.

Whipped Cream

1 cup whipping cream
3 tablespoons confectioners'
   sugar
2 teaspoons vanilla extract

For the whipped cream, beat the cream, confectioners' sugar and vanilla in a mixing bowl until stiff peaks form.

Tiramisu

3 egg yolks
1/2 cup sugar
2 cups brewed espresso
2 tablespoons brandy
1 cup mascarpone cheese
3 egg whites, stiffly beaten
2 (3 1/2-ounce) packages ladyfingers
Baking cocoa to taste

Beat the egg yolks and sugar in a mixing bowl. Add 1 tablespoon of the espresso and the brandy. Add the mascarpone cheese and beat for 5 minutes. Fold in the egg whites.

Dip the ladyfingers in the remaining espresso, reserving enough ladyfingers to line the edge of the bowl. Place 1/3 of the espresso-soaked ladyfingers over the bottom of a trifle bowl. Spread 1/3 of the mascarpone cheese mixture over the ladyfingers. Repeat the layers. Arrange the remaining espresso-soaked ladyfingers over the top.

Split the reserved ladyfingers and line the edge of the bowl. Spread the remaining mascarpone cheese mixture on top and sprinkle with baking cocoa.
Yield: 12 to 16 servings.

Favors

To make your dinner party extra special, provide a favor for each guest at his/her place. It can be chocolates, something seasonal (candy corn, cinnamon hearts), a potted plant, or even a lottery ticket.

Bread Pudding with Hard Sauce

Bread Pudding

1 loaf dried French bread
4 cups milk
1¹/2 cups sugar
2 tablespoons vanilla
    extract
3 eggs, beaten
1 cup raisins

For the bread pudding, tear the bread into a bowl. Pour the milk over the bread and let sit for 1 hour. Whisk the sugar and vanilla into the beaten eggs. Stir into the bread mixture. Stir in the raisins. Pour into a greased baking pan.

Bake on the middle oven rack at 375 degrees for 1 hour and 10 minutes. Let cool to room temperature. Cut into squares and place on a heatproof dessert plate. Spoon the hard sauce over the bread pudding and broil until bubbly. Yield: 8 servings.

Hard Sauce

¹/2 cup (1 stick) butter
1 cup confectioners' sugar
1 egg, beaten
¹/4 cup whiskey

For the hard sauce, melt the butter in a double boiler over simmering water. Add the confectioners' sugar and cook until dissolved, stirring constantly. Remove from heat. Whisk in the beaten egg. Beat until the sauce has cooled to room temperature. Mix in the whiskey.

Greek Diner Rice Pudding

4 quarts milk
2 cups white rice
3 cups sugar
1/3 teaspoon salt
6 eggs
2 tablespoons vanilla extract
1 cup golden raisins
Cinnamon to taste

Scald the milk in a large saucepan. Add the rice, stirring constantly to prevent the milk from burning. Cook for 20 to 30 minutes or until the rice is of the desired consistency but not overcooked, stirring constantly.

Combine the sugar and salt in a large mixing bowl. Add the eggs 1 at a time, beating well after each addition. Beat in the vanilla. Add the rice mixture in very small amounts at a time to prevent curdling, mixing well after each addition.

Return to the large saucepan and cook for 8 to 10 minutes. Stir in the raisins. Let cool; the rice will continue to thicken as it cools. Serve warm or cold, sprinkled with the cinnamon. Yield: 12 servings.

Cookbook Contributors

The following individuals contributed recipes, candid evaluations, kitchen time, meal time, and moral support to the creation of this cookbook. We thank them for their generous gifts of self.

Lori Ahdieh
Victoria Penske Aitchison
Mike Albano
Sally Albano
Kathy Appleton
Hansook Atkins
Rosemary Coyle Azzalina
Joanne Barnette
Marcia Barone
Patti Barry
Sharon Bell
Rosie Bencivenni
Maureen Britney
Peggy Brown
Sandra Burroughs
Kathy Calabrese
Tony Calabrese
Mark Caldwell
Jim Carey
Jolene Carey
Paula Comber
Ruth Condit
Krystina Conway
Sarah Cooper
Amanda Moss Cowan
Kathy Csatari
Lucinda Dealtrey

Karen DeLuca
Laraine Demshock
Trudi Denlinger
Jamie Dimbokowitz
Cindy DiRenzo
Laura DiRenzo
Louis DiRenzo
Robert DiRenzo
Debra Dubbs
Milano Dune
Dolly Dyer
Clare Ebner
Dan Ebner
Mary O'Hara Eichhorn
Jon Elekes
Fran Feathers
Michelle Federov
Danielle Foder
Matthew Foder
Meg Sheridan Fogarty
Lorrie Garcia
Kristen Gaumer
Ellen Harter
Kevin Hausman
Mary Ellen Hausman
Elesia Heimbecker
Bonnie Heydt

Milissa O'Hara Hoeing
Eve Hoffman
Beverly Hoover
Ginger Horsford
Sarah Hunt-Barron
Valerie Hutton
Ellen Johnson
Lynne Johnston
Julie Jordan
Pat Kesling
Maria Kinney
Linda Koontz
Kim Kozlowski
Ray Kozlowski
Booth Kral
Joan Ullman Larky
Victoria "Lala" Leach
Amy Lear
Harrison Leuckel
Nancy Leuckel
Lisa Lutz
Megan O'Hara Malicki
R. Keith Malicki
Katie McCormack
Josie McDonald
Jean McGill
Jennifer McGrath

Betty Ann McInteer
Linda McLinden
Allison Meehan
Anne Miller
Elizabeth Mitchell
Allison Moxey
Shirlee Neumeyer
Diane Nolan
Amy Normington
Edison Norton
Lynn L. Norton
Jim O'Hara
Lori O'Hara
Mary Beth Okula
Michelle Olson
Cindy Oster
Carey Patterson
Patricia Penske
Lisa Pomraning
Steve Pomraning
Rosemary B. Reese
Jill Rust
Elizabeth Sarris
Marie Savinelli-Yardley
Amy Scalici
Maureen Schenkel
Phil Schenkel
Sharon Schock
Annelise Shaffer
Bob Shaffer
Heather Shaffer

Sara Levin Shaffer
Karen Sipp
Ann Siuciak
Diane Siuciak
Greg Siuciak
Nancy Smillie
Barbara Miller Smith
Sharon Smith
Cidney Spillman
Anna Maria Stoerrle
Al Stubbmann
Wendy Littner Thomson
Cathy Tighe
Jennifer Topp
David Trimble
Kathleen Duggan Trimble
Mike Trohey
John Wagner
Kristina Warner
Alistair Westwood
Daphne Westwood
Nancy Kesling Westwood
Harry Wilson
Jenifer Whitten Woodring
Robin Wolak
Cynthia Staffieri Workman
Sheri Yenawine
Pam Zucker

We gratefully recognize the participation of the following restaurants in our community:

The Apollo Grill,
   Bethlehem
The Bethlehem Club,
   Bethlehem
The Inn of the Falcon,
   Bethlehem
The Lafayette Inn, Easton
O'Hara's Pub, Allentown

Index

Entertaining Thoughts . . .

A lighthearted collection of recipes, menus, and entertaining tips presented by

The Junior League of the Lehigh Valley
2200 Avenue A, Suite 101
Bethlehem, Pennsylvania 18017
Telephone: (610) 866-8852
Fax: (610) 866-2053

Please send _____ copies of *Entertaining Thoughts* at $19.95 each . . $ _____

Pennsylvania residents add sales tax at $1.20 each . . . . $ _____

Postage and handling at $4.00 each . . . . $ _____

Total . . . . $ _____

Name
_____

Address
_____

City   State   Zip
_____

Method of Payment: [   ] MasterCard   [   ] VISA

                      [   ] Check payable to The Junior League of the Lehigh Valley

Account Number   Expiration Date
_____

Cardholder Name
_____

Signature
_____

Photocopies will be accepted.